M000032442

The Uncommon Wisdom of
Oprah Winfrey

Donald and Laverne Philpott
505 Holly Lane
Cedar Grove
NJ 07009

The Uncommon Wisdom of

——————

Oprah Winfrey

——————

A Portrait in Her Own Words

Edited by Bill Adler

A CITADEL PRESS BOOK
Published by Carol Publishing Group

Copyright © 1997 Bill Adler
All rights reserved. No part of this book may be reproduced in any form,
except by a newspaper or magazine reviewer who wishes to quote brief
passages in connection with a review.

A Citadel Press Book
Published by Carol Publishing Group
Citadel Press is a registered trademark of Carol Communications, Inc.

Editorial, sales and distribution, rights and permissions inquiries
should be addressed to Carol Publishing Group, 120 Enterprise Avenue,
Secaucus, N.J. 07094

In Canada: Canadian Manda Group, One Atlantic Avenue, Suite 105,
Toronto, Ontario M6K 3E7

Carol Publishing Group books may be purchased in bulk at special
discounts for sales promotions, fund-raising, or educational purposes.
Special editions can be created to specifications. For details, contact
Special Sales Department, Carol Publishing Group, 120 Enterprise Avenue,
Secaucus, N.J. 07094

Manufactured in the United States of America
10 9 8 7 6 5 4 3 2 1

The Library of Congress has cataloged the Birch Lane Press edition as follows:

Winfrey, Oprah.
    The uncommon wisdom of Oprah Winfrey : a portrait in her own words
/ edited by Bill Adler.
        p.   cm.
    "A Birch Lane Press book."
    ISBN 1-55972-419-6 (hc)
    ISBN 0-8065-1894-4 (pb)
    1. Winfrey, Oprah—Quotations. 2. Television personalities—
United States—Biography. 3. Motion picture actors and actresses—
United States—Biography. I. Adler, Bill. II. Title.
PN1992.4.W56A3   1996
791.45'028'092   96-37404
[B]—DC21   CIP

Editor's Note

Compiling a list of quotations by Oprah Winfrey, one of America's most beloved entertainers, presented a unique challenge. Along with my research associate, Virginia Fay, I looked through hundreds of magazine and newspaper interviews and articles and reviewed television shows, speeches made by Oprah Winfrey, and many other sources in search of Oprah's words of wisdom. Our next task was to take the many, many quotations we found and edit them down to the ones we thought would best represent the multiple facets of her character as well as the incredibly compelling story of her life. I hope that the end result, *The Uncommon Wisdom of Oprah Winfrey,* like my previous books *The Uncommon Wisdom of Jacqueline Kennedy Onassis* and *The Uncommon Wisdom of Ronald Reagan,* presents an insightful and balanced portrait of this amazing woman.

Bill Adler
New York City, 1996

CONTENTS

Contents

Contents

Contents

Contents

Contents

Contents

GROWING-UP YEARS

Mississippi

On January 29, 1954, Oprah Gail Winfrey was born in Kosciusko, Mississippi. She describes the occasion of her conception as a "one-day fling under an oak tree."

"I was supposed to be named Orpah, from the Book of Ruth. But the midwife got the letters transposed, and I wound up Oprah on my birth certificate."

CHILDHOOD

"I was born a poor, black chile."

She once described herself as a "nappy-headed little colored girl."

"We had an outhouse. You never forget it. No matter how many bathrooms you get, you never forget it."

"The nearest neighbor was a blind man up the road. There weren't other kids. . . . no playmates, no toys except for one corncob doll. I played with the animals and made speeches to the cows."

"I used to take the cows to the pasture in the morning and feed the hogs.
    "I used to do all that. But I'm thankful because I feel like I have an edge on a whole lot of other 'talk show people.' I have experienced so many different *kinds* of things."

I've been the best talker and the best reader ever since I can remember."

On Sunday she would go to church wearing patent leather shoes:
    "I literally didn't wear shoes until Sunday. I was barefoot all the time because I lived on a farm."

"It was lonely. I had one corncob doll, I rode a pig bareback and spent most of my time reading Bible stories to the barnyard animals."

Looking at snapshots with a reporter in 1986:
    "This is the house I was born in on my grandmother's farm in Kosciusko, Mississippi. Isn't it amazing—I remember thinking what a high porch it was, and it's only from there to there. I remember, every time I jumped off I thought I accomplished such a great feat. 'Whooooo, I jumped off the porch.' I called my grandmother Momma."

"I look sad a lot. On this one I look real bad, really crazed. I did smile, though. I think I did. I was a *really* likable child and loved to kiss people and talk to them. But I couldn't because my grandmother's philosophy was children should be seen and not heard. Company would come and I would be ordered to sit in the corner and keep my mouth shut. By the time I was three, I was already talking and reading a lot. I never saw a movie and maybe twice a year I got to see TV."

"This picture is of Glenda Ray's house. This was a big treat for me, to go to her house. Glenda Ray lived down the road in a brick house and her mother was a schoolteacher and she had toys and real dolls."

At church Oprah made her grandmother, Hattie Mae, proud. She had a natural talent for recitation and performing. She recalled those times to Jane Pauley:

"I started out speaking there, and it was a way of getting love. And you know, the sisters sitting in the front row would fan themselves and nod to my grandmother, Hattie Mae. And they'd say, 'Hattie Mae, this child is gifted.' And somehow, with no education, my grandmother instilled in me a belief that I could aspire to do great things in my life."

Speaking of her grandfather, Earless Lee:

"I feared him. Always a dark presence. I remember him always throwing things at me or trying to shoo me away with his cane."

Asked whether she'd wanted to be white:

"I used to sleep with a clothespin on my nose, and two cotton balls. And I couldn't breathe and all I would do is wake up with two clothespin prints on the side of my nose, trying to get it to turn up. I wanted Shirley Temple curls; that's what I prayed for all the time.

"The reason I wanted to be white was that I never saw little white kids get whippings. I used to get them all the time from my grandmother. It's just part of southern tradition—the way old people raised kids. You spill something, you get a whipping; you tell a story, whatever happens, no matter how small the indiscretion, you get a whipping. Sometimes you get 'em saved up."

"I wanted to be a little white kid because they didn't get whippings. They got *talked* to."

HER GRANDMOTHER

"My grandmother whipped me with switches. You go and pull a little limb off a tree and you bring it in. It's what Richard Pryor described as the loneliest walk in your life—to get your own switch. Amazing, isn't it?

"You couldn't just say 'I won't do it anymore.' The other thing is, in the middle of the whippings they say, 'Now shut up. Now shut up,' and you couldn't even cry. You get whipped till you have welts on your back. Unbelievable. I used to get them every day because I was very precocious. I was always getting into trouble and I always thought I could get away with it.

"But you know, I am what I am because of my grandmother; my strength, my sense of reasoning, everything. All of that was set by the time I was six years old. I basically am no different now from what I was when I was six."

"She could whip me for days and never get tired. It would be called child abuse now."

"If I didn't get one that day, it would be saved up until Saturday because Saturday was bath-bathing time."

"I remember one day I had gotten a mighty whipping. I had gone to the well to get some water. And I was singing to myself, as I always did. Singing 'Zippity Doo-dah,' walking through the pasture, dipping my fingers into the water, just a-playing with it and splashing it all over. I did not know my grandmother had intended this to be drinking water. So I got to the house and she says, 'Girl, were you playing in that water?' I said, 'No, ma'am,' with water dripping all over my hands. She said, 'I'm gonna get you for that.' I didn't get a whipping for three days. Three days passed and I thought, 'Well, she forgot that whipping.' "

"Sure, Grandma whipped me, she sure did. But she taught me about life, and I loved her so. I'll look like her when I'm old. I'll be one of those spiritual ladies rockin' and shoutin' in church. Yes, ma'am, you'll find me in the amen corner."

"I remember when I was four watching my grandma boil clothes in a huge iron pot. I was crying, and Grandma asked, 'What's the matter with you, girl?' 'Big Mammy,' I sobbed, 'I'm going to die someday.' 'Honey,' she said, 'God doesn't mess with his children. You gotta do a lot of work in your life and not be afraid. The strong have got to take care of the others.'

"I soon came to realize that my grandmother was loosely translating from the Epistle to the Romans in the New Testament—'We that are strong ought to bear the infirmities of the weak.' Despite my age I somehow grasped the concept. I knew I was going to help people, that I had a higher calling, so to speak."

"It was my grandmother who was responsible for developing my natural talents early."

"What would've happened if I had had the kind of grandmother who, instead of beating my butt, would've sat me down to discuss, you know, my feelings over the matter?

"Perhaps I could've been more sensitive."

Speaking of her grandmother Hattie Mae, who gave her a deep and abiding faith in God and a conviction that 'he is the center of the universe":

"Once you understand that, it's all really simple."

Looking at snapshots:

"This little girl is posing because she's so thrilled to have somebody there to take her picture. . . . I don't know where our money came from. I really don't. My grandmother owned the farm and she did everything herself. She made my clothes; I never had a store-bought dress. We grew everything we ate. We sold eggs. . . . I don't know.

"I slept with my grandmother. In the big featherbed. . . . There was a well, down about a hundred yards from the house, where I had to go to get water in the morning. That was my job—to go and get the water."

Told she doesn't look as poor as she describes:

"I know. That's because my grandmother took very good care of me. And the most I can say about my mother: She believed in dressing. She's the kind of person who would dress no matter what, and she always dressed us well. It was very important to her, even though we were on welfare, to have us all dressed well all the time."

Years later, on a show about bringing up children:

"Our prisons are filled with older men who, as young men, had the living hell beat out of them. Every parent who beat them said, 'I'm doing this because I love you.' When my grandmother used to whip my behind, she'd say, 'I'm doing this because I love you.' And I'd want to say, 'If you loved me, you'd get that switch off my butt.' I still don't think that was love.

"I certainly do think that many of the whippings I received were unnecessary. I believed it at the time and [she pauses and looks toward the ceiling as she calls out] I believe it today, Grandmomma! Let me tell you!

"I really do think there's a difference just with my white friends growing up and my black friends growing up."

Referring to the caller, she adds:

"This woman is feeling traumatized because she spanked her three-year-old, when, as black children, we had a whipping every day of our lives. That's sort of like what you went through."

"Thank goodness I was raised by my grandmother the first six years, then sent to live with my mother and then with my father. Because of the various environments I was exposed to, I am better able to understand what others have gone through."

Milwaukee

When Oprah was six, she went to Milwaukee to live with her mother, Vernita Lee, who worked as a cleaning woman and was on welfare.

She was only in kindergarten a few weeks when she wrote her teacher a note:

"Dear Miss New: I don't think I belong here."

Impressed, the teacher moved her up a grade. A year later Oprah recalls:

"I didn't think it was necessary to go to second grade, so I told my teacher and was moved into third grade. I couldn't stand to be bored."

". . . [I] started speaking and reading in the churches and doing poetry and gospel. I started making a little name for myself and became an orator. People started calling me a leader in school.

"If I was playing school, I wouldn't play unless I was the teacher. Or we didn't play house unless I was the mama.

"I came from a matriarchal family so I had to be the mama and had to tell the daddy what to do!"

"When I was seven, I lived in Milwaukee with my mother. She was a roomer with some lady who was my sister's godmother or something. And I felt like I was an outcast. I don't know why mother ever decided she wanted me. She wasn't equipped to take care of me. I was just an extra burden on her."

"In first grade six white kids were going to beat me up. So I told them about Jesus of Nazareth and what happened to the people who tried to stone him. The kids called me the Preacher and left me alone after that."

Nashville

"At the end of my first grade I went to live with my father and my step-mother. I had been skipped at school and was supposed to start third grade that September. My stepmother discovered I didn't know any math and was going to be in big trouble when school began. So my entire summer I spent learning my times tables. My stepmother was real tough, a very strong disciplinarian, and I owe a lot to her because it was like military school there. I had to do book reports at home as well as in school and so many vocabulary words a week. That's what we did."

"On Monday mornings I led devotion in class, with graham crackers and milk."

"Not only did I have homework from school, but homework at home! Plus I was allowed an hour a day to watch television, and that hour was always before *Leave It to Beaver* came on! I hated that! But, you know, it is the absolute reason I got my first job in radio. I was hired on nothing else other than that I sounded good."

One of Oprah's fondest memories from that first year spent with her father and stepmother were the career goals:

"I wanted to be a missionary for the longest time! I was a missionary for Costa Rica, let me tell you. I used to collect money on the playground every single day of the year. I was a maniac."

Milwaukee II

"I moved back to live with my mother when I was nine. The reason was that my mother would say, 'Come live with me. I'm gonna get married and we're all gonna be a real family.' This guy she'd been dating for years, he's also the father of my brother. So that's why I stayed; I wanted a normal family. It never worked out, though. I wanted a daddy when I was in Milwaukee. I wanted a family like everybody else because I was going to this school where kids had mothers and fathers. I used to make up stories about my mother and my dad. I told the biggest lies about them because I wanted to be like everybody else.

"In this environment I felt really ugly because the lighter your complexion, the prettier you were. My half sister was lighter and she got all the attention and I thought it was because she was the prettiest. I was the smartest, but no one praised me for being smart. I was teased because I was always sitting in a corner reading; people made fun of me for that. And I felt really sad and left out. My books were my friends."

When Oprah's career began to take off, she claimed she'd been raised in poverty. She told one magazine:

"We were so poor we couldn't afford a dog or cat, so I made pets out of two cockroaches. There were lots of roaches available. You wanted pets, all you had to do was go in the kitchen at night and turn on the lights. You could find a whole family of them. So I would name them and put them in a jar and feed them . . . like kids catching lightning bugs. I called them things like Melinda and Sandy. You can't catch lightning bugs in the wintertime, so I'd keep roaches in a jar. Now I'm repulsed by the idea."

"At thirteen I saved up enough money to buy a dog, but my mother threatened to give him away for pooping on the floor, so I ran away."

Again, looking at snapshots with a reporter:

"This was on North Main Street in Milwaukee. I'm thirteen. This was when we were our poorest. I had just started in this school called Nicolet where everybody else was white. It's when I realized the difference. Up until that time I'd been poor but didn't know it. My sister and brother and I slept in one room, and my mother had another room. That was it. I was terribly troubled. I couldn't understand why I couldn't have the smallest things, like pizza money. And so I made this plot to run away.

"I was going to go and stay with my girlfriend. I put all my things in a shopping bag and went to my girlfriend's house and there was nobody home. [She laughs.] I didn't check with her, and they were out of town. There was nobody there. Now what am I going to do? I was very determined.

"I just started walking downtown. And I saw Aretha Franklin getting out of a limousine. I started crying and told her I'd been abandoned. I guess I looked really pitiful. I said I'd been abandoned and could she please give me some money so I could go back to Ohio (I liked the sound of Ohio). And so she did. She gave me a hundred dollars and I went and stayed in a hotel. It was the saddest time in my life. After I ran out of money, I called the late Reverend Tully and asked him to help me go back home. I told him everything that was going on in my house and how bad

I felt. So he took me back to my house and gave my mother a lecture, which really pleased me."

A junior-high questionnaire asked, "What will you be in twenty years?"
  Oprah responded, "Famous."

HER MOTHER

"My mother was the best-dressed maid ever known to woman. You know how you see women going to work at the nice white people's houses wearing slacks? My mother would put on high heel shoes and her suede skirt and go stepping'.

  "It was very important for her not to look the part. She'd get her hair done and go to work."

"I started acting out my need for attention, my need to be loved," as she analyzed it later. "My mother didn't have the time. She worked every day as a maid. She was one of the maids on those buses. I was smart—and my mother, because she didn't have the time for me, I think, tried to stifle it."

Oprah says she felt angered that her mother had to work as a maid, but adds:
  "I adjusted to it. It's really no big deal. It is no big deal. I think people become what they can in life. You do what you can."

"My mother, like everybody else's mother, I think, did the best she could, the best she knew how to do. It's like the character I play in *Native Son*. She says to her son, after he's been convicted of murder, 'Son, I did all I knew how.' And many mothers are that way. They never hug because their way of saying 'I love you' is that they get up and go to work every day. I was the kind of kid who would have benefited from hugging. But she doesn't understand that, and I can't change it."

"Not getting the attention from my mother made me seek it in other places, the wrong places."

"She was a young black woman on welfare struggling with three kids, so I know she acted out of her own pain."

"I forgive her for any anger and hostility, and she forgives me."

"I think I was angry with her for a long time because I thought in some way maybe she knew [about the abuse] and didn't want to do something about it. But I've made my peace because I think that my mother . . . gave me all that she had to give."

CHILDHOOD SEXUAL ABUSE

"Well, my own experience was that when I was a nine-year-old, I was left for a day in the care of a nineteen-year-old cousin and I was raped that day. While living with my mother in Milwaukee, I was repeatedly sexually molested by a, quote, 'family friend.' And when I was fourteen, I was molested by an uncle."

"I remember being at a relative's house and I had been left with a nineteen-year-old cousin and he raped me. And I knew it was bad and I knew it was wrong, mainly because it hurt so badly. He took me to get ice cream and to the zoo afterward, and he told me if I ever told, we would both get in trouble. So I never did. It was in the summer of my ninth year. . . . So that's why I weep for the lost innocence. I weep for that because you are never the same again."

"I had no idea it was a sexual thing, because I didn't have a name for it."

She was grateful for the attention, thankful when he bribed her with presents.
    "I sold my silence for an ice-cream cone and a trip to the zoo."

Looking at a picture taken when she was nine:
    "Oh. This is the person who's going to be abused. When this was taken, I'd already been raped. . . . It's in the fall and I was raped that summer. That is the first thing I thought when I saw this picture yesterday. I thought, oh, this is the summer it happened.
    "To this day I haven't told anybody his name. He was nineteen. They had put me in bed with him. There was only one bed and I had to sleep with him. Can you imagine? I didn't know anything about sex that summer, but when I started school in September, someone told me for the first time where babies come from, and I remember, after that, thinking, that whole year, that I was going to have a baby. I was afraid every day that I was going to have a baby. I didn't tell anyone about it because I thought I would be blamed for it."

"Every time I had a stomachache, I thought I was pregnant and asked to go to the bathroom so if I had it nobody could see.

"That for me was the terror. Was I going to have it, how would I hide it, all the people would be mad at me, how could I keep it in my room without my mother knowing?

"I know what it is like to lie in bed and know that other person is there, and you are pretending you are asleep, hoping he won't touch you."

"It didn't happen anymore with that one person, but it happened over a couple of years with my mother's boyfriend. I was an open target living in that environment."

"It happened over a period of years, between nine and fourteen. It happened at my own house, by different people—this man, that man, a cousin. I don't like making a big deal of it. I remember blaming myself for it, thinking something must be wrong with me. I started to act out, looking for love in all the wrong places."

She was also abused by a favorite uncle:

"I started to feel like I had a banner on my head. I adored this uncle. Just adored him. And I could not, in my mind, make him be the bad guy."

As she recalled years later:

"We had started this conversation, we were talking about boys in school, the conversation went to kissing boys and 'Have you kissed boys?' and the next thing I know, he was taking my panties off. My uncle, whom I adored."

"What caused me to be continually sexually abused was being in a family that I didn't think would support me if I told.

"And also the shame that resulted from being sexually abused . . . the shame and the guilt and the fear. . . . I realized I stuffed all those feelings."

She said in one frank interview:

"I blamed *myself*. I was always very needy, always in need of attention, and they just took advantage of that. There were people, certainly, around me who were aware of it, but they did nothing."

"What it does to you, you cannot come out of it without being touched in some way. What it did for me is that it made me a sexually promiscuous teenager. And it's very confusing, because if it's the first time in your life anyone has ever shown you any kind of affection or attention, you confuse that with love, and so you go searching for it in other places. . . . And you get it any way you can. And so I used to run away from home and I used to bring boys home when my mother wasn't there. And cause all kinds of problems for myself. Until I was fourteen. And then sent to live with my father, and that ended it. Just ended it."

In a 1988 *People* magazine interview she discussed her teenage promiscuity after being molested, and she said that the sexual attention from boys and men was pleasing and she liked it:

"When that article came out, the response I got was, how dare you say that you liked it? Which wasn't what I was saying at all. If someone is stroking your little breasts, you get a sexy, physical feeling. It can be a good feeling, and it's confusing, because you then blame yourself for feeling good, not knowing that you had nothing to do with that kind of arousal. A child is never to blame."

"I was twenty-two or twenty-three years old when I did an interview with someone who had been sexually abused. It was the first time it occurred to me that this thing that had happened to me had also happened to other people. I hadn't told anybody until then because I thought I was the only person it ever happened to and I thought it was my fault because afterward it happened repeatedly by different people."

She was willing to share her inner feelings with her guests and audience. In 1985 she was interviewing a victim of sexual abuse. Suddenly she spoke up:

"The same thing happened to me. The fact that I had all these unfortunate experiences permeates my life."

Later she said:

"I just wanted to say 'I understand.' I hadn't planned to say it. It just came out."

On her famous admission of being molested as a child:

"We were doing a show on the subject, and it was something—the phones lit up with calls from women all over the country saying the same thing had happened to them as girls. The guest I was interviewing started crying, and I started crying and told for the first time that it had happened to me too."

On her revelation of her childhood abuse:

"I had several young adults on the show who said they were sexually abused by relatives when they were small children.

"As they talked about their experiences, revealing the emotional pain and trauma they had suffered, I had the courage to also admit that I had been sexually abused when I was very young.

"It wasn't something I had prepared to do beforehand. But after hearing every story, I suddenly felt compelled to reveal my own story and I did.

"People everywhere congratulated me. It was good therapy, a catharsis. I no longer had to live with this horrible secret, and I knew it could help others who had suffered the same way."

"If you have been sexually abused and kept silent, you keep putting yourself in situations later in life where you can be abused again: by your boss, or by friends who take advantage of you, or by men who say they're going to call, then lie to you, cheat on you. You set yourself up for that."

"The saying of it on the air for me was really quite, not only cathartic, but very therapeutic, in just getting the words out, but I still had not released all of the shame. And I tell you, I did a show last year [1990] with Truddi Chase, who was a victim of just severe sexual and child abuse, and in the midst of telling her story, I . . . started crying uncontrollably. I could not stop. It was all of my own stuff coming out. It was my own stuff coming out on national television."

On child abuse:

"Well, you can't break it until you're aware of how much damage it really does. Andrew Vachs, a leading child advocate and attorney, has said this . . . many times, and I so much agree with him, that if you abuse a child, that child will either turn on himself or herself or turn on the world.

And that's really the reason, you know, we know that the prisons are filled with people who commit so many crimes and there's such, you know, grave drug problems in this country. These are all children who developed no sense of self-value and grew up to be adults who turned on the world. So I think if we can start to expose and to eradicate the problems stemming from the way we treat children, we can begin to heal ourself as a nation. I really believe that."

"I think what most people do . . . and that is not being able to shift the blame to the adults because when you are a little girl or a little boy growing up, many times the adults are the ones who make you feel that you are the one to blame. And I remember being told by my uncle, who was the last person to molest me, that, you know, I had asked for it and that if I ever told, that that's what would be said. And so I didn't tell until, you know, I was, you know, much older, until I was an adult."

"I remember in Baltimore years ago the first time I ever heard somebody talk about it on TV. I couldn't believe that it had happened to somebody else. And I was so tempted then—I was twenty-two years old the first time I heard it. And I hadn't told anybody about my own. And I—and I was like—I wanted to meet with the woman afterward but didn't have the nerve to say, 'This happened to me, too.' So years later, when I had the confidence on my own show to do it, I did it."

"Every bad relationship I've ever been in is the result of my having been abused.

"What stops the cycle of abuse is awareness."

"I never talked about my feelings, any more than I did when I was molested and raped, then worried that a stomachache meant I was pregnant. Until I was in my twenties, I never told a soul. My relationships with men were disastrous. Whenever I trusted someone, he abused me. It happened several times, even by my cousin's boyfriend. When I gathered the courage to tell my mother's side of the family the truth, they criticized me for airing my dirty laundry in public."

1987

On her family's reaction to her sexual abuse:

"What makes me resentful is their unwillingness to accept my feelings. They now want to pretend as though our past did not happen. I'm now the favorite daughter, favorite sister, as you can imagine."

In 1978 she attempted to discuss her childhood abuse with her family:

"But my mother said she didn't want to hear it, so I never brought it up again."

The abuse fueled her need for control:

"It's all about fear, all my problems, even my weight. When I'm heavy, I feel safer and more protected, although I don't know what I'm trying to protect any more than I know what I'm so afraid of. Food for me is comforting. It also calms me. I find its results, however, very distressing and a real monkey on my back."

1992

"I never moved on. I still haven't. I was, and I am, severely damaged by the experience. All the years that I convinced myself I was healed, I wasn't. I still carried the shame, and I unconsciously blamed myself for those men's acts. Something deep within me feels I must have been a bad little girl for those men to have abused me."

1992

"I made the commitment because it's part of my own healing. I think it does no good for me to have had all of this horror in my life and not be able to grow from it."

"You lose your childhood when you've been abused. My heart goes out to those children who are abused at home and have no one to turn to."

She spoke to a Senate Judiciary Committee on child abuse in 1991:

"Everybody deals with their pain differently. Some become over-achievers like me, and others become mothers who kill."

"When I get tears in my eyes about the whole question of sexual molestation, I always think that it's not for me. I only cry when I think about it happening to other people."

SCHOOL DAYS

"I felt it happen in the fourth grade. Something came over me. I turned in a book report early and it got such a good response, I thought, 'I'm gonna do that again.'"

"Mr. Gene Abrams used to see me reading in the cafeteria. He got me a scholarship to Nicolet High School."

In the late sixties Oprah was part of an experiment whereby desegregation was to be obtained by ferrying children from mostly black neighborhoods to mostly white suburban schools. She recalled:

"I was feeling a sense of anguish, because living with my mother in Milwaukee, I was in a situation where I was the only black kid, and I mean the only one, in a school of two thousand upper-middle-class suburban Jewish kids. I would take the bus in the morning to school with the maids who worked in their homes.

"The life that I saw those children lead was so totally different from what I went home to, from what I saw when I took the bus home with the maids in the evening. I wanted my mother to be like their mothers. I wanted my mother to have cookies ready for me when I came home and to say, 'How was your day?' But she was one of those maids. And she was tired. And she was just trying to survive. Her way of showing love to me was getting out and going to work every day, putting clothes on my back, and having food on the table. At that time I didn't understand it."

"It was the first time that I was exposed to the fact that I was not like all the other kids. In 1968 it was real hip to know a black person, so I was very popular."

"The kids would all bring me back to their houses, pull out their Pearl Bailey albums, bring out their maid from the back, and say, 'Oprah, do you know Mabel?' They figured all blacks knew each other. It was real strange and real tough."

"I *realized* I was poor then."

Mothers would enthusiastically encourage their children to invite Oprah home with them after school:

"Like I was a toy. They'd all sit around talking about Sammy Davis, Jr., like I knew him."

"I'd get in the bus in the evening after school and go home, and the white kids would go to the pizza parlor and drive their *cars* and stuff!

"And after seeing how the other half lived, I started having some real problems. I guess you could call me *troubled*—to put it mildly."

"For the first time I understood that there was another side. All of a sudden the ghetto didn't look so good anymore.

"I used to take three buses to get back home twenty miles every day.

"It was like going back to Cinderella's house from the castle every night."

"I wanted to have money like the other kids. They were always saying, 'Let's go to the pizza parlor, Opie.' 'Let's get shakes, Opie.' "

Teachers

"I wanted to be my fourth-grade teacher for a long time. I wanted to be Mrs. Duncan. Fourth grade was the turning point in my life—I discovered long division!"

When Oprah was about twelve, she was far ahead of the other kids. A special teacher, Eugene A. Abrams, took an interest in her, getting her into a program called Upward Bound. He helped her get a scholarship to enter Nicolet High School in Fox Point, a Milwaukee suburb.

When he passed away in 1991, Oprah said that he had been "one of those great teachers who had the ability to make you believe in yourself. I know there are many former students like myself whose lives have been touched. We're going to miss him."

Family

"Growing up, I acted differently when being raised by my mother than being raised by my father.

"I would break curfew. I'd stay out. I'd run the streets. Because I knew I could get away with it. You know why? Because my mother would say, 'If you come in here late again, I'm gonna break your neck!' Well, I knew she wasn't gonna break my neck. So I would do whatever I could get away with. On the other hand, my father didn't even have to say it. You just knew that if you did it, you'd be shot. You knew if you came in late, you would die!"

"It's interesting how people have different ways of showing love.

"So many of us grow up with June Cleaver on our minds. We think that's the way it is. So, as a child, if your mother doesn't have milk and cookies waiting for you when you get home, you think that everybody else's mother is doing that and they're packing nice little lunches with love and saying, 'Go off and have a great day, Suzie!' When that doesn't happen, you feel traumatized in many ways."

Oprah's later relationship with her mother and half brother, Jeffrey, wasn't good, although she helped them out financially after she became successful. Oprah had been paying Jeffrey's rent, then stopped, but raised the amount she gave their mother. Vernita Lee did not pay Jeffrey's rent at first, then gave the landlord a check that bounced. The landlord kicked Jeffrey out and sued Vernita for the money. When Oprah found out about the bounced rent check, she said:

"My mother is getting dunning notices from this landlord and never once tells me what's going on. What am I going to do with these people? I'm heartsick."

"I'm not going to get any more involved in Jeffrey's financial situation. He should be taking care of himself. I'm torn over these financial situations that both he and my mother are involved in, but it's not my responsibility to be bailing them out each time they get into a jam.

"It may make me seem like a hard person. They can say I'm ignoring my family and all, but you've got to look at the total picture. All the years that I went without a family, and now they want me to be part of a family I don't even know."

Re her half sister, Patricia Lee, in treatment for her drug problems:

"She's still my sister. I can't abandon her. I cut off the money—not my love."

1989

On supporting her mother and sister financially:

"It's so hard when there's money involved. It's so hard. It wasn't until I bought my sister a house [and the sister protested because Winfrey won't pay her electric bills], that I realized you cannot buy people their personal freedom. No matter how much you do, there is always an excuse. She is over her drug problem, which is tremendous, so I say, 'What you need now is the discipline just to get up and go to work every day.' I've told her I'll support her going back to school, but she says, 'Education doesn't work for me. If you'd just give me the money, I could start my own restaurant.' "

1995

"Yesterday I went to dinner at my mother's house and there were cousins and uncles and friends and they're bringing friends I don't even know who want me to help them with their careers. 'Can you help your uncle with this and your sister with that...?' It's like they think I'm the Godfather or something. I was so stressed at the end of the day. Everyone's so needy. They *need* so much. And I'll give them whatever I can; it's no skin off my back.

"We all had prayer yesterday before I left. And I asked the spirit of God to touch everyone in the room and allow them to understand that each of them had the power to take control of his life. But do you think they heard it? Nooooo."

1986

In March 1990 Oprah's half sister betrayed a deep family secret to the *National Enquirer*—the story that Oprah had given birth to an illegitimate child when she was fourteen. The story was picked up by *Parade*. Oprah told *Parade*:

"That experience was the most emotional, confusing, and traumatic of my young life."

"Everybody in the family sort of shoved it under a rock. Because I had been involved in sexual promiscuity, they thought if anything happened, it had to be my fault."

Nashville II

Recalling her mother's attempt to have her put in a juvenile detention center in 1968 (fortunately for Oprah, the Milwaukee system was over-burdened, and her mother was told they'd have to wait two weeks):

"I remember going to the interview process where they treat you like you're already a known convict and thinking to myself, how in the world is this happening to me? I was fourteen and I knew that I was a smart person; I knew I wasn't a bad person, and I remember thinking, 'How did this happen? How did I get here?'

"My mother was so fed up with me at the time that she said, 'I can't wait two weeks. You've got to get out of the house now.'

"I was sent to live with my father in Nashville, and he changed my life."

"I'm grateful to my mother for sending me away. If she hadn't, I would have taken an absolutely different path in life."

Her father worked as a barber and owned a grocery store:

"I had to work in the store, and I hated it—every minute of it. Hated it. Selling penny candy, Popsicles. But without him—even with all this potential—I never would have blossomed."

"Not getting the attention from my mother made me seek it in other places—the wrong places, until my father came and got me from my mother in Milwaukee and took me to Nashville, where he lived. His discipline channeled my need for love and attention into a new direction."

HER FATHER

She says her father "straightened [her] out":

"My father turned my life around by making me see that being your best was the best you could be. His love of learning showed me the way. Reading gave me hope. For me it was the open door."

"When my father took me, it changed the course of my life. He saved me. He simply knew what he wanted and expected. He would take nothing less."

"I was a child who was always in need of discipline. I have a great father who used to tell me, 'Listen, girl, if I tell you a mosquito can pull a wagon, don't ask me no questions. Just hitch him up.' That's the kind of dad I had, who was a very, very stern disciplinarian. It's because of him, I believe, I am where I am today. I was badly in need of direction."

"The most important men in my life have been positive. My father was a hardworking man who owned his own business and took care of me."

"My dad really held me in with a tight rein. Without his direction I'd have wound up pregnant and another statistic. I was definitely headed for a career as a juvenile delinquent."

"I often talk about him being so strict, but he was so strict because he knew what he had to deal with."

"When my father said, 'If you don't bring *As* into this house from school, you can't live here,' he meant it."

"I knew exactly what I could and what I couldn't get away with. I *respected* his authority."

"He was the kind of father who said, 'Be home by midnight, or, by God, sleep on the porch!' And he meant it."

Oprah and Stedman visited her father in Nashville:
   "We slept in separate bedrooms. I would absolutely not even try it. I wouldn't even dare try it! Are you kidding? We had bedrooms at opposite ends of the hall."

Vernon Winfrey accepted Oprah as his daughter right from the first:
   "Emotionally I still feel disconnected. I feel like these were some nice people [Vernon and his wife, Zelma] who took me in. Because my mother named several people [men who might have gotten her pregnant with Oprah] and my father was one of them. He took responsibility because I could have been his. To this day there has never been an official test. And over the years people have said, 'Well, I don't know if he really is your dad.' But he is the only father that I know. He took responsibility for me when he didn't have to. So my father saved my life at a time when I needed to be saved. But we're not, like, bonded."

"I retired my mother, who is eighteen years older than I, and my father is twenty-one years older than I. And I offered to retire him. But he has his barbershop in Nashville. He doesn't want to. He'd miss the guys. And he is the kind of person—I bought him the big Mercedes. And he said to me—But he wasn't going to drive it to work, because he doesn't want the people in the barbershop to think he's, you know, bragging or anything."

In 1987 Oprah gave the commencement address at Tennessee State University and received her diploma. She endowed ten scholarships in her father's name.

Later that year she threw a party in Chicago. During the program she thanked everyone who had helped her, including her father, Vernon Winfrey, a small man who blew her a kiss from his seat.

"He's a skinny little man. I didn't take those genes from him."

Referring to the incident where a Tennessee State student claimed Oprah's father had forced her to touch his genitals when she went to his barbershop to ask for help in obtaining scholarship money (the charges were dismissed for lack of evidence):

"I knew, knowing God as I do, that that would happen. But I kept asking, 'Why has this happened and what am I supposed to learn from it? What is he supposed to learn from it?' "

The lawsuit at first upset her terribly:

"You have to understand, when I was a kid, the biggest infraction my father ever had was when he went through a period where he played checkers a lot and my stepmother was crazed about him playing those checkers for a dollar a game. I remember her pulling me out of bed one night and saying, 'We are going up the street because your father is up there at Mr. Haynes's house playing those checkers.' That was as big as it ever got. So for this to have happened . . ."

She also felt some guilt

"because if he didn't have me for a daughter, that could not have happened to him."

"I was really worried about him for a while because I thought it was going to break his spirit."

"My father still doesn't know who I am. So I think something had to happen for him to see he can't continue to be Mr. Friendly-Friendly."

"I am appalled that his reputation is on the line because of an unsubstantiated accusation.

"My father, Vernon Winfrey, is one of the most honorable men I know. In his professional and personal life he has always tried to do what is right and help people. Since my childhood, he has set excellent standards that helped me succeed."

"My father still hasn't grasped the enormity of my celebrity status."

Beauty Contests

~~~

Still in her teens, she entered the local Miss Fire Prevention contest:

"I entered it as a fluke. I entered because at the time, we were Negroes—we hadn't gotten black yet. So I was the only Negro in the 'Miss Fire Prevention Contest.' I certainly never expected to win because, why would I? And I won. I said I wanted to be a journalist, like Barbara Walters."

"When the judges asked me what I wanted to do with my life, I was going to say, 'Become a fourth-grade teacher.' But I had seen Barbara Walters that morning on the *Today* show, and it just popped into my head to say I wanted to be a journalist."

She told the judges:

"I believe in truth, and I want to perpetuate the truth. So I want to be a journalist."

She was named Miss Fire Prevention in Nashville at age seventeen:

"I know it's not a biggie, but I was the only black—the first black—to win the darned thing. I went on from there and entered the Miss Black Nashville contest, because I'd gotten all this publicity for being the first black who ever won the Miss Fire Prevention contest."

And then Miss Black Tennessee, in 1971:

"I didn't expect to win, nor did anybody else expect me to. There were all these light-skinned girls—vanillas—and here I was a fudge child—real dark-skinned. And Lord were they upset, and I was upset for them. Really I was."

"Beats me, girls! [she told them when it was all over and the ruffled egos had all been stroked]. I'm as shocked as you are. I don't know how I won, either."

On becoming Miss Black Nashville and Miss Black Tennessee:

"I had marvelous poise and talent and could handle any question, and I would always win on the talent part, which was usually a dramatic reading. I could—I still can—hold my own easily. Ask me anything, and my policy has always been to be honest, to tell the truth. Don't try to think of something to say, just say whatever is the truth."

"I was raised to believe that the lighter your skin, the better you were. I wasn't light-skinned, so I decided to be the best and the smartest."

"I won beauty contests not because I was beautiful. I won beauty contests because I was talented. I always would win on talent and would want to apologize to all the pretty girls. I mean, at the end of the contest, I'd want to say, 'Look, I don't know how I got it. I don't know. I guess it was that poem I did.' But I was thinner, yes. Much thinner."

On the Miss Tennessee beauty contest:

"You could see my *bones*."

College Years

"It was a weird time. This whole black power movement was going on then, but I just never had any of those angry black feelings. I tried to do the 'Hey, brother' bit, but it was a sham. Truth is, I've never felt prevented from doing anything because I was either black or a woman."

On her years at Tennessee State:

"No one's asked me about my psychological health at that time. Frankly I felt that most of the kids hated and resented me. They were into black power and anger. I was not. I guess that was because I was struggling just to be a human being. While they called me an 'Oreo,' I remembered Jesse Jackson saying, 'Excellence is the best deterrent to racism.' So I pushed myself. In high school I was the teacher's pet, which created other problems. I never spoke in dialect—I'm not sure why, perhaps I was ashamed—and I was attacked for 'talking proper like white folks,' for selling out."

On the attitudes of her classmates:

"They all hated me—no, they resented me. I refused to conform to the militant thinking of the time. I hated, hated, hated college. Now I bristle when somebody comes up and says they went to Tennessee State with me. Everybody was angry for four years. It was an all-black college, and it was in to be angry. Whenever there was any conversation on race, I was on the other side, maybe because I never felt the kind of repression other black people are exposed to. I think I was called 'nigger' once, when I was in fifth grade."

"Race is not an issue with me. It has never been an issue with me. In school, when the other black kids were organizing a bloc vote for student council, I couldn't work with them because I thought their candidate wasn't the best qualified. I was ostracized then; they called me 'Oreo.' "

"People see me and they see that I am black. That's something I celebrate. But I don't feel it's something I need to wave a banner about, which used to cause me all kinds of problems in college. I was not a dashiki-wearing kind of woman."

In 1987, TSU alumna Oprah was asked to give the commencement address. She agreed, but insisted that she finish her course credits first so that she could finally get her own degree. She told the audience that her father had said she would never amount to anything until she got that degree. When she got the diploma, she waved it and said:

"See, Daddy, I amounted to something."

CAREER MOVES

The News Business

~~~~~

When she was seventeen, the black radio station that sponsored her in the Miss Fire Prevention contest hired her to work part-time after school as an afternoon news anchor:

"I had gone by the station to pick up my Longines watch—the contest prize—and one of the guys had a tape recorder and asked me if I'd ever heard my voice on tape. When he heard my voice, he called in the news director and said, 'Hey, listen to this kid read.' "

She was hired on the spot.

Oprah confided to Judy Markey of *Cosmopolitan*:

"I really agonized. I was a horrible writer, and I just broke down and cried with all those crime and fire stories. But I stuck it out, because I figured one day it could lead to a talk show."

She knew she was a part of the push to help minorities find jobs when she was hired to anchor on WTF-TV in Nashville:

"Sure, I was a token. But, honey, I was a very happy token."

"When I was doing television in Nashville, I was given a stand-in job for just one day filling in on one of those local talk-show community-affairs programs that air at two in the morning. I remember being given the opportunity, just on a temporary basis, and thinking this is what I'd like to do."

Baltimore

After working at WTVF in Nashville, she moved on to be coanchor on WJZ in Baltimore:

"I really wasn't cut out for the news. I'd have to fight back the tears if a story was too sad."

"I just didn't have the proper reportorial detachment."

"It was not good for a news reporter to be out covering a fire and crying with a woman who has lost her home. I knew from the beginning that I was only a performer. To a great extent that's what telling the news is—a performance. But newspeople will tell you that it's not *performing* at all."

"I'd never read the news in advance, and it made the news director angry. I'd be reading something and break in to say, 'Wow, that's terrible!' All my reactions were getting to be real. It was a kick to me. It wasn't organized."

"So it was very hard for me to all of a sudden become 'Ms. Broadcast Journalist' and not *feel* things. . . . You're at a plane crash and you're standing right there and you're smelling the charred bodies, and people are coming to find out if their relatives are in the crash. And they're weeping, and you weep, too, because it's a tragic thing.

"So I recognized that I had a problem. But I still remained a reporter. That's what I was hired to do. For a long time I continued as a reporter and an anchorwoman."

"I was a restrained self. The thing about being a cohost on a show is that it's like being married. And in ninety-nine out of a hundred cases in talk shows, the female is the one who gives."

"Cohosting is like being married. I don't think you could have found a better team than Richard [Sher] and me.

"I never considered myself funny. Richard was always the funny one. I was always the straight man."

After a totally disastrous attempt to make her over as news coanchor, she was exiled to a morning talk show:

"They put me on the talk show just to get rid of me, but it was really my saving grace. The first day I did it, I thought, 'This is what I really should have been doing all along.' "

"In Baltimore I was put on the talk show because I was twenty-two years old and somewhat naive, and I was coanchoring the six o'clock news! And the chemistry left a lot to be desired. I was so naive I just thought you could go on the air and do the best you could.

"It did not work. I was called in and told so on April Fool's Day, 1977. So anyway, my 'demotion' was just a way of getting me out of the way.

And I did this talk show—I think I was interviewing the cast from *All My Children* and the Carvel ice-cream man—big time, you know, I'm telling you. I finished that show, and I thought, 'This is it. This is what I was born to do. This is like breathing.' "

"And they didn't know what to do with me. And that's really how I ended up doing a talk show."

During the height of *People Are Talking*'s popularity, a local Baltimore community newspaper interviewed Oprah Winfrey and Richard Sher and wanted to know if they ever argued:

"If I don't like something Richard's doing, I tell him.

"Put it this way, sometimes he can be difficult. But I understand a lot."

THE MAKEOVER

During her time at WJZ-TV in Baltimore:

"I lived my life to please other people. They told me my nose was too wide, my hair too thick and long. I couldn't even decide what kind of hair I wanted. They came to me and said, 'Your eyes are too far apart, your nose is too wide, your chin is too long, and you need to do something about it.' So they sent me to New York, to a chi-chi, poo-poo, lah-de-dah salon—the kind that serves you wine so when you leave it doesn't matter what you look like.

"So this Frenchman put a French perm in my black hair. I was the kind of woman at the time—this was 1977—I sat there and let this French perm burn through my cerebral cortex rather than tell this man, 'It's hurting.' I told myself, 'Oprah, be a good sport. This man must know what he's doing.' What he did was burn my hair right off."

"I felt the lotion burning my skull, and I kept saying, 'Excuse me, this is beginning to burn a little.' They kept saying, 'Oh, just a few more minutes.'"

Within a week all her hair fell out:
   "You learn a lot about yourself when you're bald."

"They wanted to make me a Puerto Rican. Or something. What I should have said then, and what I would say now, is that nobody can tell me how to wear my hair. I've since vowed to live my own life, to always be myself."

She was interviewed for the August 1986 issue of *Good Housekeeping*:
   "If you're black and walk into a place where everybody's speaking French, *run* in the opposite direction."

"There were no wigs big enough for my head—it's twenty-four inches around—so I had to walk around wearing scarves for months. I was devastated, and I had to find some way to get back my self-esteem. Which is hard when you're a black, bald, out-of-work anchorwoman."

She told Mike Wallace on *60 Minutes*:
   "Yeah. I had a French perm, and it all fell out. Every little strand. I was left with three little spriggles in the front. [Wallace laughs.] Funny to you. They tried to change me, and then they're stuck with a bald black anchor-

woman. I went through a real period of self-discovery, because you have to find other reasons for appreciating yourself. It's certainly not your looks."

LIFE AND "DEATH" IN BALTIMORE

In Baltimore, Oprah dealt with sexual harassment on the job:
  "This man was constantly propositioning me and talking foul language. I was young and impressionable, and there was no excuse for his behavior. He made me feel uncomfortable and creepy. I stayed away from him and vowed to get away as soon as I could. I was so grateful when I got the chance to go to Chicago."

One person who provided support during her crises in Baltimore was reporter Lloyd Kramer:
  "Lloyd was just the *best*. That man loved me even when I was bald! He was wonderful. He stuck with me through the whole demoralizing experience. That man was the most fun romance I ever had."

After Lloyd Kramer moved to New York, she eventually became involved with a man she said her friends had warned her to stay away from:
  "I was a doormat."

A long-term romance of four years ended when she left Baltimore for Chicago:
  "That forced me to grow up fast. I learned that you can't change other people. Only yourself."

"Suicide" Attempt

❦

Of her "suicide note," written in September 1981:

"I don't think I was really serious about suicide, but I wrote my best friend a note—it was a Saturday, around eight-thirty. I'd been down on the floor, crying. I told her where my insurance policies and papers were, and I asked her to take care of my plants. I came across the note just lately—this is the first time I've talked about it—and I cried for the woman I was then."

"I had so much going for me, but I still thought I was nothing without a man. I'd had a relationship with a man for four years—I wasn't living with him, I've never lived with anyone—and I thought I was worthless without him. The more he rejected me, the more I wanted him. I felt depleted, powerless. Once I stayed in bed for three days, missing work; I just couldn't get up.

"Sad, ain't it!"

"That suicide note has been much overplayed. I couldn't kill myself. I would be afraid the minute I did it something really good would happen and I'd miss it."

"I was so adamant about being my own person that I wouldn't go for counseling. Then it came to me: I realized there was no difference between me and an abused woman who has to go to a shelter, except I would stay home. It was emotional abuse, which happens to women who stay in relationships that do not allow them to be all that they can be.

You're not getting knocked around physically, but in terms of your ability to soar, your wings are clipped."

During a 1987 show on teenage suicide, she admits she once considered suicide:
"Over a man. Can you believe that? Never, never again."

Drug Use

The drug incident occurred when she was in her early twenties and until she revealed it on her show in 1995, it was, she says, "my life's great secret, the thing I was second most ashamed of, the first being the child that I had [as an unmarried teenager]."

Oprah said her drug use occurred while she was an anchorwoman on a TV news show, during her 1973–76 stint at Nashville's WTVF-TV.
Oprah acknowledged the contradiction of her life back then:
"I had a perfect, round, little Afro, I went to church every Sunday and I went to Wednesday prayer meeting when I could . . . and I did drugs."

On revealing her past drug use on her show:
"What I learned from it is the thing that you fear the most truly has no power. Your fear of it is what has the power. But the thing itself cannot touch you. What I learned that day is that the truth really will set you free."

"What I know is that the spirit of God inside all of us . . . a lot of people believe the drug is stronger than the power of God . . . there is nothing greater than the spirit within you to overcome it."

From an article by Patrice Gaines of *The Washington Post*, who appeared on the show:

"I very much related to your story. I had always thought I was more addicted to the man than the drug, but I could never say it out loud—I was always ashamed. I would never admit that I handed over my power to a man, to the point that he could influence me to do anything for him."

Turning to one of the guests who had admitted smoking crack, Winfrey said:

"I relate to your story so much because of what Patrice just said about being on a television news show."

"It's my life's great big secret. It was such a secret because—I realize [with] the public person I have become—if the story ever were revealed, the tabloids would exploit it and what a big issue it would be."

"I was involved with a man in my twenties who introduced me to the same drug that you've been talking about and, like Patrice, I always felt that the drug itself is not the problem but that I was addicted to the man. I can't think of anything I wouldn't have done for that man."

Reflecting on this difficult period in her life:

"And I've often said over the years . . . in my attempts to come out and say it, I've said many times I did things in my twenties that I was ashamed of, I did things I felt guilty about, but that is my life's great big secret that's always been held over my head."

"I understand the shame. I understand the guilt. I understand the secrecy. I understand all that."

"I was not addicted. It was something I did for a short period with a particular boyfriend. I thought he communicated better with me [when they smoked cocaine], I thought he was more open and more loving. I had heard of Richard Pryor freebasing [the actor who burnt himself almost fatally in the process], but when it was offered to me, I didn't know that's what it was.

"There are some people who knew that it was in the book [an autobiography she was working on] and had been threatening to go to the press. So because I am a public person, more and more shame became attached to the secret."

From an article by Patrice Gaines in *The Washington Post*, January 13, 1995:

"I would have felt like a hypocrite, not saying [I had smoked cocaine], talking to people about baring their souls and standing there like I didn't know what they were talking about. When Charmaine said, 'I wanted to come here because I knew you would be honest and straightforward with me,' I knew I had to say something.

"My heart was beating fast. I could see the tabloids before me. But I would have felt like a fraud if I hadn't said it."

"It was very freeing. I will never have to worry about this again."

On *The Ed Gordon Show*, May 30, 1995:

"Since I knew that I had this secret about having done drugs with a boyfriend years ago, I always knew that there was a possibility of it being exploited by the tabloids and being betrayed by a family member or an associate, close associate whom I'd shared it with. So the fear of it is something that had caused me to be, you know, live this kind of secretive life. And then I was absolutely, Ed, insulted is the word. I was insulted and surprised that anybody would think that this thing that has been my greatest shame, my big dark secret, the thing I least want anybody to know about me, I mean, I was like, how could anybody think I would do *that* for ratings? I was insulted by that."

Winfrey said she told Stedman Graham early in their relationship that she had used cocaine at one point in her life:

"I was concerned about how it would affect him, but he knew from the start it was one of the secrets I was having trouble dealing with and he encouraged me not to let it be a big fear. He's never taken a single drug and doesn't drink alcohol."

Chicago, Chicago

"I really grew up there in Baltimore, you understand. I felt natural and cared for there. But it was time to move on. I made a deliberate choice about where to go. Los Angeles? I'm black and female and they don't work in L.A. Orientals and Hispanics are their minorities. New York? I don't like New York, period. Washington? There are thirteen women to every man in D.C. Forget it. I have enough problems."

"When you have finished growing in one place or time, you know. Your soul tells you when it's time to move on."

Asked to send a résumé and audition tape to Chicago:

"Well, I'm the most disorganized person on earth, and maybe I'm gonna get that accomplished in this lifetime. I'm tired of worrying about it.

"I am the kind of person who—in all my years of television history— has not put one résumé or tape together. I always figured when it's time to go, somebody will call me."

"I thought, 'Oh, my goodness! What am I going to say? What am I going to do?' I went to a résumé expert."

Because of Oprah's news experience, she was tapped by WLS-TV in Chicago to coanchor the trial run of a new program, a move she wasn't thrilled with:

"I didn't want to do the news and had made it clear that I didn't want to do it.

"That was part of the growth to get to where I am now. I am a better interviewer and talk-show host because of it. All of those fires, chasing ambulances, plane crashes, political hearings, and gas and electric company meetings—all that stuff—helped to get me where I am. It also helped me to shut people up when I need to. That's part of the art, too. It's give-and-take, because people come on and they want to tell you what they want to tell you. And you want them so they can tell what you want them to tell you. So you have to be able to say, 'Okay, we've heard enough about that now,' without actually saying it."

"My first day in Chicago, September 4, 1983. I set foot in this city, and just walking down the street, it was like roots, like the motherland. I knew I belonged here."

"I remember walking to the corner and gettin' blown down by the wind, and I said, 'Well, this is a sign I'm supposed to go back to the hotel!' "

"From the day I landed here [for an audition at Channel 7], I loved this city. So I thought, okay, I'm probably not going to get this job, since they're never going to hire a black, overweight female, so I'll send my résumé to all the other stations. Then if they turn me down, well, I'll try their publicity departments. True, I'd never done publicity before, but I'd try anything. Because I just knew that I was supposed to be in Chicago."

Oprah told *Ebony* her initial reaction to auditioning for hosting duties at *A.M. Chicago* was:

"You can forget it. They're not going to put a black woman on at nine in the morning—not in Chicago, not on prime-time morning television."

"So when I was interviewed for my first job, I told my boss, 'You know I'm black, and that's not going to change.' He said, 'Yeh. I'm looking at ya.' And I said, "Yeah, well, and I have this weight problem, too.' And he goes, 'Yeah, well, and so do I. So I'm not going to hold that against you.'

"I was expecting to come here and be picketed out of the city. To have people scream at me. None of it ever happened. But it doesn't mean that

I don't—in every fiber of my being—know that I am black and understand what that means in this country."

Oprah became host of WLS-TV's *A.M. Chicago* show in January 1984. Everyone warned her against tackling the mighty Donahue:

"They said I was black, female, and overweight. They said Chicago was a racist city."

Oprah told P. J. Bednarsky of the *Chicago Sun-Times*:

"I had my own little game plan for Chicago. In one year I'd walk down the street and people would know who I am. In two years people would watch me because they'd like me. In three years I'd gain acceptance—you know, I'd see Phil Donahue getting a pizza and I'd say, 'Oh, hi, Mr. Donahue. I watch your show sometimes.' "

"This is my year. I mean it's tre-tre-double-mendous! It's my time to have fun, fun, FUN!"

1986

"There aren't a lot of black people in the Chicago media, and I'm the only one doing what I'm doing. When I came on the air here, it was like you could hear TVs clicking on all over the city."

She told P. J. Bednarsky:

"I'm gonna be okay, 'cause I've been here six months and I'm still feeling great. It's the happiest time of my life, and you know, usually you don't feel good for six straight months. I'm just wondering, when is something horrible going to happen."

When she first got to Chicago and found success with her show:

"I thought I was handling the stress just fine. The show was going well. I was doing great. Everyone told me how easy I made it all look.

"But underneath I was terrified. So at night I'd sit up alone in my room at the Knickerbocker Hotel and order French onion soup by the gallon. 'Oh, and could you fry up a cheese sandwich to go with that?' That's how I was handling things."

"People are no different in Podunk than in Chicago. [Here] they may dress differently and live in high-rises, but when it comes to human desires and human hopes, we are all the same. One of the reasons I enjoy doing shows like today's is it lets people know they are not alone. Every woman who has felt that sense of rage inside will recognize herself by seeing the other women, and will hopefully get help."

"I'm glad to be doing the show from the Midwest. People here can still be shocked."

Rush Street, just a few blocks from Oprah's home, is one of Chicago's most well-known streets:

"It's my street. It's a great place to meet people, especially when you're one of the most well-known people in Chicago. You're never alone."

She commented to David Brenner:

"I love Chicago. I do think it's the best city in the world, and I've seen half of it, but I think it's the best.

"Chicago's a lot like New York. It has the energy of New York, but it's not quite so overwhelming. We can still be surprised in Chicago."

"I become totally excited when I just think about Chicago. Because being here has meant the recognition for me that I received in other places, but it has meant more because of the kind of city Chicago is. I call it 'cosmopolitan country.'"

"Chicago is one of the most racially volatile cities anywhere. Our success there shows that race and sex can be transcended."

"I love this town! You can quote me on that. It's got such a great energy . . . its own vibes. It's a civilized New York. The people are great and friendly."

"This cold was awesome. It was *serious* cold. I thought I was delirious in the streets! I tell you, Negroes weren't built for this kind of weather! We start praying for the motherland!"

"I'll never leave Chicago, the best city in the world. In fact the reason we have bad weather sometimes is just to scare people away from the idea of moving here."

"You know what, if it wasn't twenty-below-zero windchill outside, everybody in the world would live here, because this is the greatest city in the world. Greatest city in the world, except for the weather."

BIG SISTERS

In 1986 she and her staff formed a Big Sister group with two dozen teenage girls from the Cabrini-Green Housing Project in Chicago:

"I shoot a very straight shot: 'Get pregnant and I'll break your face! Don't tell me you want to do great things in your life and still not be able to tell a boy no. You want something to love and to hug, tell me and I'll buy you a puppy!' "

"One girl on the Cabrini-Green show said her goal was to have lots of babies, so she'd get more money from welfare. We have twenty-four in our group. Maybe we'll save two."

"When we talk about goals, and they say they want Cadillacs, I say, 'If you cannot talk correct, if you cannot read or do math, if you become pregnant, if you drop out of school, you will never have a Cadillac, I guarantee it! And if you get any *Ds* or *Fs* on your report card, you're out of this group. Don't tell me you want to do great things in your life if all you carry to school is a radio!' "

DONAHUE

"Everybody kept telling me that it was going to be impossible to succeed because I was going into Phil Donahue's hometown. So, you know, I'd eat and eat. I'd eat out of the nervousness of it all . . . and then people were saying, 'There are going to be pickets outside your door.' "

"I used to watch him all the time. I'd tape *Donahue*. There was a point where I noticed I was doing the same thing with the microphone that he does and I said, 'Phil does that.' One day on the air I said, 'Hey, would you help me out here?' And then I said, 'Oh boy! I've been watching too much of Phil.'

"I have the greatest respect for him, though. I learned how to do what I do because of him."

Her show debuted nationally in September 1986, competing with *Donahue* in many markets. An article in the September 1986 issue of *Savvy* detailed the differences between Oprah's and Donahue's styles. A Multimedia staffer explains that Donahue, for instance, would not greet a guest like Bishop Desmond Tutu of South Africa with a hug. Oprah laughs at this comment. She recently bumped into the bishop. They'd never met before, but she hugged him and he hugged her back:

"Bishop Tutu wouldn't hug Donahue."

In 1987 she won the Emmy. She thanked Phil Donahue for blazing the trail for their kind of show:

"One of the biggest moments of my life came right then. After I thanked him, he came up to my table and he kissed me, and that's when I knew that it was all media-contrived and he didn't hate me at all! 'You deserve it, you deserve it, you deserve it!' he told me."

"He'd do nuclear disarmament much better than I would. He'd have all the stats, be very thorough, and I'd be accused of being overemotional."

"Without Donahue [my] show wouldn't be possible. He showed that women have an interest in things that affect their lives and not just how to stuff cabbage. Because of that I have nothing to prove, only to do good shows. . . . I say, he's the king and I just want a little piece of the kingdom."

In February 1987 Oprah was topping Donahue's ratings. After she was awarded an Emmy that year, she told the audience:

"I would like to thank Phil Donahue, because twenty years ago when Phil Donahue started, people who were managers in television thought women were only interested in mascara tips. . . . Phil Donahue showed them women are interested . . . in living the best possible lives."

"I like Phil Donahue, but I have to admit, it feels good to beat him. For the longest time I couldn't go about doing my job without people saying, 'Yeah, you're good. But are you as good as Donahue?' "

1987

Again in 1993 she won the Emmy as Outstanding Talk Show Host and again paid tribute to Donahue for creating the form:

"He's the master at what he does. He made it possible for there to be an Oprah."

Donahue made the move to New York shortly after Oprah began beating his show in the ratings. Oprah refuses to take credit (or blame) for his moving.

"I didn't run him out of Chicago—Mario did. But I did run him out of his time slot. *Yipppeee!*"

"It's just that here we are stomping him in the ratings, you know, and suddenly—he's gone! It was maahvelous!"

"Yes, he's the man. And when Phil first started out, Phil was the first to understand that the woman at home was an intelligent, sensitive, knowledgeable person who wanted to know more than how to bake Toll House cookies. So, I mean, Phil, in the beginning, really set the standard. Of course we all know that the standard has changed. But I will say that unless there are those of us who are willing to take a stand—and I think that, of course, everybody says this is the most powerful medium on earth, the vehicle of television—unless you're willing to stand for something, we're all going to fall together. And I do believe that Phil certainly is one of those people who also understands that with the airwaves comes a sense of responsibility."

Re the cancellation of Donahue's show in New York (1995):

"I'm sorry that he's off [in New York] because I think he's one of the few that stood for quality television."

On the demise of Phil Donahue's show:

"If I were Phil, I would have gotten out a long time ago. I was at his twenty-fifth-year celebration and thought, 'You won't be seeing me with twenty-five candles on a cake.' "

Oprah's statement, January 1996, when Phil Donahue announced that he was retiring from his talk show:

"I'm very, very sorry to hear this. Phil really opened the door to this genre, and for that I am grateful. I have said from the very first day of my show, if there hadn't been a Phil, there wouldn't have been me. We'll miss you, Phil."

ON HER WORK

She doesn't like to work from a script:

"It just doesn't work for me. It throws me totally off balance. How can I ask a question if I already know the answer? I look like I'm faking it."

"Back in May, when we were working so hard on the show, I said to our crew, 'You have to take time to regroup, rejuvenate, restore your energies.' I gave them all a two-month vacation. But I didn't do that for myself. I worked all summer filming [*There Are No Children Here*]. And later I'm thinking, 'Why did I do that? I have to take time for myself.' So that was the lesson I learned this summer. Because Stedman finally just went on vacation without me. He took his daughter. And she enjoyed the French Riviera very much, thank you. And I worked in the projects."

1993

"Well, I've always had lines drawn. There are always things I wouldn't do. Earlier in my career I was more concerned about not doing anything that would cause any harm. You know, I would say, 'Well, we don't want to do this because we don't want that to send the wrong message, and you're speaking to millions of people every day, so let's make sure we don't do anything that causes any harm.' I'm now more concerned about using my life and my show to really have a message of goodness. I think, you know, for myself, having evolved emotionally, physically, financially, spiritually, that the spiritual dynamic of life is really the most important thing to me."

"The truth of the matter is I get paid very well for doing this job. However, I would have done the job that I'm doing now for absolutely free because I love the work. . . . I'm glad I'm not doing it for free, but I would have done it for free and taken a night job in order to do it. So I think the love of the work . . . that's why I feel badly for people who work every day and hate what they're doing."

"For ten years I've been doing shows about dysfunction, and what I found is the reason we have the kind of society that we have is related to the way we have been parented. The way we stop the dysfunction—to save our world—to save our children—is to help parents understand what is wrong in our homes, our schools, our communities, and do something about it."

1995

"I think it was necessary to get those things out of the closet. I think it was necessary to get the country talking."

Re what she considers her most interesting show topic:
    "I've done several thousand. The ones that have mattered the most have been when I've been able to change the way people think for the better. For instance over the years I've received hundreds of letters from battered women who saw a show we did and found the courage to get out. 'How to Protect Your Kids from Strangers' was a goose-bump show for me 'cause I knew we were saving kids. I have lots of those. I get goose bumps a lot."

Oprah surprised some fans last year when she dropped in at a Brooklyn home and asked:
    "You don't mind if I use your bathroom, do you?"

"I've always wanted to go by somebody's house, just stop in around four o'clock, and see if they're watching *The Oprah Winfrey Show*. And these women were watching."

"Parenting is the toughest job in America. This season I want to talk to parents who are raising children who go to school, who aren't drug addicts, who are growing up to be honest people. I want to applaud *those* parents, and empower the kids and parents who are getting it right."

HOME SWEET HOME(S)

Describing her condo, undergoing renovations:
   "A mess—it's like a bomb dropped on it."

1985

In the summer of 1986 she moved into an apartment formerly occupied by real estate mogul (and wife of former New York governor Hugh Carey) Evangeline Gouletas-Carey. Oprah told *Cosmopolitan*:
   "Evangeline left behind some nice touches—a wine cellar, a crystal chandelier lighting up the inside of my closet, and a marble bathtub with gold dolphins for spigots.
   "I didn't break my promise. . . I bought the apartment as my present [to herself for becoming a millionaire by age thirty-two]."

"Of course there's not a stick of furniture in the place now, because my decorator threw all my old stuff out."

"It is so great living up here. The sun rises off the lake in the morning, right through this window—and it's a joy to my soul! Good Lord, I do feel blessed!"

On cleaning up for the cleaning lady:

"I don't want her to think a pig lives here."

Once, while relaxing on her farm porch in Indiana, she spoke to a lost wanderer who had gotten stuck in the mud down the road from her:

"He said, 'Hey, I was going down the road to see Oprah Winfrey's house. Don't she have a house down here?'"

The multimillionaire television star looked the stranded traveler deep in the eyes and said, in her best down-home accent:

"I believe she do."

"Outside my house in Indiana is a big field. I have visions of just rolling down the hill in the grass. And the moment I get a spare hour, that's exactly what I want to do. I want to see if it feels as good as I've been fantasizing it would."

HER RESTAURANT

In February 1989 she opened the Eccentric, a restaurant in Chicago. She was totally involved, even refilling the toilet paper in the bathrooms:

"I have to check the bathrooms every half hour, they're very strict about that. Besides peeling the potatoes, I do get to make the Perrier sodas—my favorite. But I won't be answering phones, because I can't tell you how to get here."

THE OPRAH WINFREY SHOW

In the Beginning

In 1984, WLS-TV put the little-known Winfrey against Phil Donahue in the nine A.M. slot. She felt the heat:

"I kept thinking, 'If things go bad, it's my buns out there.'"

She says she succeeded there because she did her show solo:

"Up until now I've always been paired with somebody else. The thing about working with a coanchor or a cohost is that it can be stifling, like a bad marriage. Somebody always has to surrender to the other person. And usually the person doing the surrendering was me. . . . I feel good about where I am right now. I feel I've earned the right to be here."

"When I began my talk show, I was so thrilled to have the opportunity that I never thought much about the tremendous influence TV could have. Now I feel both the power and the enormous responsibility that comes with it."

National Syndication

◦━◦

"I want to be syndicated in every city known to mankind."

1986

Talking about the show going national:

"It'll do well. And if it doesn't, I will still do well. I will do well because I am not defined by a show, you know. I think we are defined by the way we treat ourselves and the way we treat other people. It would be wonderful to be, you know, acclaimed as this, you know, talk show host who's made it. That would be wonderful. But if that doesn't happen, there are, you know, other important things in my life."

"I have this fear they may promote me as the Second Coming," Oprah told Greg Bailey of the *Nashville Banner*. "The hype is used to get people to tune in. Once they do, they'll make up their own minds about me. They're not all going to love me."

On doing a promotional tour to promote the newly syndicated show:

"I'm always interviewing people on my show who are in the midst of these types of promotional tours. I'm used to asking the questions. The only time I've answered this many questions was during *The Color Purple*. We did forty-two interviews in one day. It's like going through therapy. I normally don't sit around and analyze what I do, where I am, and the path that got me here. Now I find myself talking about things I never wondered about before."

Talk Show Hosting

"I'm a natural interviewer. I don't do a lot of preparation. I don't like to work from a script. It confuses me. I'm best when I can sit down, have a conversation, and develop some sort of insight."

"Doing talk shows is like breathing to me. It's been a living hoot!"

"Every day the job is a challenge. It's simply important to me to be the best I can be. And in this business if you're good, it speaks for itself."

"It bothers me when we're accused of being sensational and exploitive. We are not. We are a caring group of people. [pause] Sometimes we make mistakes."

1986

When Liz Smith asked Oprah how she kept up the pace, she laughed and said:
    "I want to seize the time while it is here, and I love what I'm doing."

1989

"I'm really proud of this television show. Every day my intention is to empower people and my intention is for other people to recognize by watching our show that you really are responsible for your life. I think I can be a catalyst for people beginning to think more insightfully about themselves and their lives."

1991

"I think a show, any show, can endure as long as we are flexible and truthful. It won't endure if we start faking ideas or moments, or pretend that we're something we're not, or create an atmosphere that we believe people will buy into. Living on our guts seems to be the key, in addition to telling the truth. Television is the greatest medium in the world, and I think those of us who work in it are in a blessed position. We have a responsibility to enlighten, inform, and entertain, if we can. And as long as we do that, and do that with proof in mind, we won't fail. Success is about being honest, not only in your work but in your life. And if you let that theory carry through in your work, then you have no problems."

Oprah told P. J. Bednarsky of the *Chicago Sun-Times*:
"What comes naturally is what works, so I just keep doing it. Most talk show people ask talk show kinds of questions. They're formal. They sit with their legs crossed. They *behave* themselves."

"I am exactly the same way out there as I am here talking to you. No different. You have to let yourself be vulnerable, let people see you as something other than a broadcaster."

"When people watch television, they are looking to see themselves. I think the reason why I work so well as I do on the air is the people sense the *realness*."

"My greatest gift is my ability to be myself at all times, no matter what. I am as comfortable in front of the camera with a million people watching me as I am sitting here talking to you."

"I usually *don't* do any homework. I really have learned that for me and my style of interviewing, the less preparation I do, the better—because what everybody is now calling Oprah's success is me being spontaneous, and that's all it is."

"I feel embraced by the camera. Like I'm doing exactly what I should be doing."

"Those two seconds after an interview ends, when the camera pans the set for a two-second close, are crucial. You have to keep going on with a guest, not ignore him or her. And you have to tell what went on during the commercial break. People want to know. They want you to be human."

"I reached the point where I said whatever was on my mind, I approached the show as a surrogate viewer. What could a viewer ask next? I went with the flow of the conversation instead of analyzing where I *wanted* to go. I loved to be surprised on the air."

"I believe that good communicative television should be a give-and-take. You give something to the audience and they give back to you. So I expect my audience and my guests to be as open as I am."

"I think the only differences between all the shows are the hosts actually and what the hosts bring to the show, because my personality is different than Sally's, and Phil's is different than mine. What we bring. You bring all your stuff to that particular hour, to those moments, and what you have to bring to those moments is what makes the moments different. It really is."

"I look at the ratings every day . . . and ours happens to be the number-one talk show, and so I track—I track our numbers and I normally don't look at what they're doing. It doesn't matter to me what they're doing. It doesn't matter to me what they're doing because, even if we did the same things, and we all end up doing the same things, we do them differently. So, if Phil gets a guest or Sally gets a guest, it's not, like, 'Oh, they got the guest,' because what they might do with a guest is not what I might necessarily do with a guest. My philosophy has been, if you take time to look back at the other guy, the energy that it takes to look back at everyone else, if you're running the race, causes you, sometimes, to lose your place. So it's straight ahead."

"If I say, 'Oh, nice,' about seven times in the same show, things aren't going well."

"I just taped two shows. Don't ask me what they were. I've been crying over something, but I forget what the show was.

"It's how I don't lose my mind—by not taking it home with me. I don't need to bring home other people's dysfunctions. I have my own dysfunctions."

1995

"To me it's more than a show. I mean, the fact that I'm called a talk show host is, I guess, a compliment, but it's more than a show to me. It's a way of being able to touch people's lives and make a difference in their lives. And I—you know, I don't know what everybody else is doing, but that's why I do it. I'd do it for free."

How Oprah responds to criticism:

"It depends. If I feel the criticism is justified, I respond well, and I use the criticism to grow from, and I let it work for me. If I feel that people are just talking out of the sides of their heads, and it's unjustified, or that a person has made a prejudiced judgment or an incorrect perception about my character, then I get upset."

"That talk show is the foundation on which all the rest of this was built. I'll not let it slide or ever lose control of it. I love doing that show. It lets people know they're not alone and it lets me be myself. It's the easiest thing I do all day. It's certainly easier than acting."

1990

"No. I won't do it the rest of my life and I don't even think I will do it as long as Phil has done it or—I mean, because, my . . . life has been such that, once I have done all that I can do in a particular area, I usually . . . that pattern has been I move on to whatever the next thing is. I don't know what the next thing is. Right now I'm doing it until 1995, and then we'll see. I don't know."

From an article in *Time* magazine (June 6, 1994) on the "Oprahization of the jury pool" and how talk shows affect people's perception of crime and punishment:

"What happened to you in the past is a part of who you are today. If, in the process, we have made people think that people are not responsible for their lives, then that is a fault."

GUESTS

"I don't really have a big-name-guest kind of talk show. I'm more interested in people who have overcome some personal tragedy, or who have something to offer in terms of spiritual or emotional development. People out there think that I'm their girlfriend; they treat me like that. It's really *amazing*. I think that happens because I feel like I am. I feel that there's a common bond we all share."

To a housewife-prostitute who was explaining how she was contacted to go to "work":
   "We thought all those beepers were doctors! You're sitting in the theater and all those beepers are going off—and we thought they were all *doctors!*"

Re a 1985 show with female members of the Ku Klux Klan:
   "I was reading the paper and I said, 'Let's get the Klan girls on.'"

"What you must understand is that when the show is over, those people are still going to be Klan girls, and I'm still going to be Oprah. You can only hope to expose racism for what it *is*."

"We had a black father on talking about what he had gone through to protect his daughter, and during the show I remember thinking this does more good than all the shows you could ever do about skinheads and KKK members and racism in which you say, 'Listen to us. This is why we are angry.'

"If I could just get black women connected to this whole abuse issue . . . I hear it all the time from black women who say, 'Well, he slapped me around a few times, but he doesn't really beat me.' We are so accustomed to being treated badly that we don't even know that love is supposed to really feel good."

1995

"There have been moments on this television show when people have said things that—that made me cringe. We had wives on with husbands, who—and the husbands were having an affair and we had the three of them on—and a husband said on the air that his girlfriend was having a baby. And his wife didn't know about it. It was a moment that I thought should not have happened. And I—and I—I said to her, 'I'm sorry that your husband said that to you on television. You should not have had to hear that on TV.' "

"From the beginning my philosophy has been that people deserve to come and to leave [my show] with their dignity. I never did what you see on the air today—nowhere close to it—because I never wanted people to be humiliated and embarrassed. And that is why I will not accept any kind of responsibility for the crap that we see on TV every day."

HER AUDIENCE

"She's out there, putting the laundry in" [was the way Oprah phrased it]. "Sometimes I'll just say, 'Hold on, I'm trying to get your attention.

I know you just took the roast beef out and you're trying to thaw it out.' I'm really fascinated by what people *do* in their lives all day. I could have a discussion all day with just a housewife, saying, 'What do you do?' "

"I'm *not* one of them. I say to them, 'I could not do what you do.' I can't bake a roast. I have not been in a grocery store for two years. The last time I went grocery shopping, I went on a fresh-vegetable kick. I spent sixty-three dollars on fresh vegetables. I looked in the refrigerator one day and nearly died. I saw broccoli in there that had hair all over it and was moving. I called Security for help."

"I'm not organized enough, I never made a bed. I figure I'll be back in it in twelve hours, so what's the point?"

"When people watch television, they are looking to see themselves. I think the reason why I work as well as I do on the air is that people sense the realness."

"I am those women. I am every one of them. And they are me. That's why we get along so well.

"White women stop and tell me, 'Everybody says I remind them of you.' And I say, 'But I'm much taller.' It crosses racial barriers."

On her arrival at the show, passing lines of people waiting to get in:

"I know what they're saying, 'That her? I think that's her. Nah. Can't be her. She wouldn't be comin' here lookin' like that.' "

"They're really opening up. Showing gutsiness. I want them to feel they can ask anything when they're in that studio."

Oprah takes time out to greet each member of her studio audience:
    "People want me to come to everything. Barbecues, picnics. One woman wanted me at her daughter's graduation. Last week a woman said her parents were celebrating their fiftieth anniversary. Could I come to that? Another lady knows I like potatoes and she just wanted me to come over and sit and have a little potatoes and talk!"

To the studio audience:
    "Y'all look nice and fresh and bathed."

"I love it. They get up, they get dressed, and they come here with the intention to be on this show. I respect that."

From *Entertainment Weekly*, September 9, 1994, when asked, *Will audiences still tune in if you're not doing sensational stuff?*
    "All it takes is a little courage. I'm going to risk having people call it soft or having people say, 'Her show is slipping,' when you drop a tenth of a point. That really irritates me. What's happened over the years is that we've become our own standard to beat."

SUBJECT MATTER

To Kay Gardella of the New York *Daily News*, 1989, speaking about plans for the show:

"We'll do fun things and have on lots of celebrities. But things I'll never do is invite skinheads on the program, members of the KKK, or do a show on devil worshipers or sadomasochism."

"Rather than putting on a diet expert, we get a panel of people struggling to lose weight. Rather than interviewing a psychiatrist, we get people who've contemplated suicide to talk about depression."

On a show discussing holiday blues, Oprah spoke of making calls on New Year's Eve:
   "You know what? I used to call up the operators and ask them how they were doin'. I called the fire departments, the operator, all the people I knew were on and say, 'Hey, how ya doin'? Happy New Year!' "

"The porn show wasn't *about* the social issues. We do the shows people want to see, and I usually follow the mood of the audience. I was curious, they were curious. I asked every little thing we wanted to know.
   "If I had to do it over again, I would not have been as loose as I was. I learned you should always do the honest thing, tell the audience you're as stumped as they are, go to a commercial if you're speechless!"

"I don't want to oversimplify issues. That's a worry obviously. But I think by making sure we bring in the right experts and having some kind of resolution in the individual shows we can, over the course of a season or two, show people ways to change their lives, to make themselves happier."

1993

Promo for her show:
    "Can a yeast infection lead to AIDS?"

Killing the above promo:
    "No, we're not going to go with this. I don't want to be responsible for causing a panic in America."

On an *A.M. Chicago* show discussing agoraphobics:
    "We had given out a number and this woman called the number, but no one there was able to help her because she lived too far away and they were going to charge her all this money."

The woman called Oprah back and said she didn't know what to do next.
    "I talked to that woman for two weeks straight until I found someone to help her. Finally a minister friend of mine talked her out of the house. She had been in the house for two years."

"I won't have people yelling and screaming and trying to humiliate one another."

"Let me just say this, because talk shows get a bad rap, all the time, about doing these sensational things. But we also do some incredible shows that make a difference in people's lives. We did a show with children of divorced parents, with children crying, because it was the first chance they had to express their feelings about it. We did a show with people who were terminally ill and won't be around six weeks from now. We did a show with women who had been dumped by their husbands. . . . With all the poking fun of it and everything, which I know critics like to do, but to the people that these things happen to, it's very serious."

Answering critics who call shows like hers exploitative:

"It's interesting to me that I'm called a talk show host, because I understand in my heart that there is something deeper, stronger, and more important going on with the people who are affected by the show."

"People make fun of talk shows because we do transsexuals and their parents. But I feel if something is going on in the world and it's happening to somebody, maybe somebody else is interested in it. I truly think you can do anything with good taste."

When asked, *What was your most frightening show?*

"It was a show we did on satanic cults. There was a call from a fifteen-year-old boy who had been part of a cult for ten years. He said he had witnessed human sacrifices and knew that one day he would have to sacrifice himself. He was going to a local high school and was still an active member of this cult. What is frightening about that is to realize that it is not just an idea you have in your head, but that satanism is prevalent, and we as a society are so unaware of it."

"Nothing gets booked if I don't want it. We are a team; but if I don't want to do it, it doesn't make sense to book it, because a lot depends on my interest and energy."

Oprah told her TV viewing audience on February 9, 1987:

"We bring you today to Forsyth County, Georgia, just thirty miles north of Atlanta, which in the past few weeks has gained the reputation of being a hotbed of racism.

"Our sole purpose in coming here is to try and understand the feelings and motivations of all-white Forsyth County. That's what we do every day on this show, explore people's feelings."

"I feel there are still so many issues that our country must deal with right now, most importantly those involving how we treat our children."

1995

On battered women as a show topic:

"Do not book this guest or this expert or this subject again. I cannot talk about this anymore. I am tired of battered women coming on this show, or anybody else's, who are not willing to take responsibility for themselves.

"I think five, ten years ago it was necessary to hear battered women talk about what was happening to them. Now I say to them, 'What are you going to do about it? What are you willing to do to change it?'

"In my earlier years I was really just trying to not cause any harm and if I could do good that was good, too. Now I am intentionally out to get people to think differently about themselves, their lives, and I'm intentionally trying to do good. And I think that there are just absolute forces of good and evil in the world, and even more so now than ever before."

Doing a show about guns and gun-related incidents:

"I want to raise America's consciousness."

From *Day One*, January 5, 1995, in an interview with Forrest Sawyer, who asked, *Is it fair to say that for all the good that the openness you bring to your program has done, people are now unseemly in their desire to lay out every-thing, for no particular good, just to put it out there?*

"I think that we are to a great extent, we have served as a catalyst for that. But, you know, my intention in the beginning was to get people to come to terms with the truth of themselves. And this show really has evolved as I have."

From *Ebony*, July 1995:

"The greatest responsibility I feel is to my creator and what I try to fulfill for myself is to honor the creation. The fact that I was created a black woman in this lifetime, everything in my life is built around honoring that. I feel a sense of reverence to that. I hold it sacred. And so I am always asking the question, 'What do I owe in service having been created a black woman?' "

CHANGES IN HER SHOW

"We've grown in the past ten years, the audience, the show, and I. And I want the shows to reflect that growth—even if our ratings go in the tank. I plan for this season to be different."

"I'm not going to be able to spend from now until the year 2000 talking to people about their dysfunction. Yes, we are dysfunctional. Now, what are we willing to do to change it?"

1994

"We call it spectacle TV—it's hard to compete with that."

1995

"What kind of a world do we paint for schoolchildren who see the bad news stories on TV?

"They see a world filled with depravity, with brutal murder, with heinous crimes. Is it any wonder that they're so cynical? Is it any wonder that so many people feel more helpless, less in control of their destinies in such a harsh world?

"I now know that people don't need to hear about dysfunction as much as they need to be restored. We need resolution and restoration . . . not just on daytime talk shows but in the media as a whole."

"When I started doing talk in 1978, Ginny, a producer would say, 'Oh, my Gad! We got the guest to cry in segment one! She cried!' That was my goal. Now I'm more interested in people keeping their dignity. 'Tell me why you're crying. Gather yourself together. If what you're telling me is going to make you cry, then stop telling me.' I'm not interested in that."

"The time has come for this genre of talk shows to move on from dysfunctional whining and complaining and blaming. I have had enough of people's dysfunction. I don't want to spend an hour listening to somebody blaming their mother. So to say that I am tired—yes, I am. I'm tired of it. I think it's completely unnecessary. We're all aware that we do have some problems and we need to work on them. What are you willing to do about it? And that's what our shows are going to be about."

1994

From *Entertainment Weekly*, September 9, 1994, when asked, *Is some of what you've been going through part of the reason you want to do softer, less sensational shows?*

"I resent the word *soft*. Get that down. I want to stand for something of value. That's why I won't do films or TV with acts of violence. Some of my nieces and Stedman's daughter were visiting me recently, and they were watching TV. This woman was being stalked and they were sitting there peeling an orange watching this like I used to watch Andy Griffith, hardly noticing it. I said to them, 'That is you on the screen, every time a woman is raped, killed, that is you, and that you can sit here and peel an orange, I am insulted.' And they said, 'How is that us, Aunt Oprah?' "

The tenth season of *The Oprah Winfrey Show* started in September 1995, with a new theme song by Paul Simon and a new hairdo on Oprah:

"I think we did a really good job of pulling ourselves away from the 'trash pack' last year. Ten years ago I was just grateful to be on television. Now I feel a greater sense of commitment and responsibility to the work that I'm doing."

"I can't wait to see the show open every day, just to hear the song."

"You know, I'm forty-one years old. I feel there are a lot of people who have grown up with me—grown up along with the show. They're into self-improvement as well. So we want to give people something they can come away with every day. For me it doesn't make sense to do any of this unless it's going to matter."

"I want to do responsible television."

1994

On changing the focus of her show away from the confrontational stories of her competition and toward more uplifting stories:

"It's never been clearer to me that the positive direction we're headed is the right way to go."

1995

"I do not believe that our numbers are down one point or not because we have taken a more committed view of our television show. I believe it's because there are too many talk shows."

"I try to take the high road because I just got tired of talking to people in their dysfunction. I just did. How many more years can you blame your mother?"

"What really is the driving force for me now are those moments when I know that I've reached somebody."

"I try to use this show as a voice for raising consciousness, for doing good, for letting people see themselves in a way that makes their lives better. So that's what I intend to continue to do with the show."

"Under no circumstances do I intend to move backward. Life to me is about moving forward. We're going to take the high ground. And if people watch us, that's terrific. And if they don't, then maybe you need somebody else to host the show."

ON SIGNING TO RENEW THE SHOW
THROUGH THE 1997–1998 SEASON

In 1993 she had considered quitting:

"I was at the gym and I actually saw one of our shows, which I rarely do. I watched, and I had the same feeling I had four or five years ago, when we had the skinheads on. I thought, 'What good is this doing anyone?' I realized that I wanted my show to be my voice to the world."

"I kept saying to the producers, 'We need better ideas, we can't keep doing the same shows we've been doing. I can't keep doing it.'"

"I say this every day at the producers' meetings, that I'm moving in the direction where I'm going to pull myself out of the game. Not necessarily out of the talk show, but everybody will know that I'm not even competing with those guys."

"I waver every day. I waver from week to week. I never started out to do it for the money, but I've certainly made enough money. So the question becomes whether we will be able to do the kind of show that we need to do. Can I do the kind of TV that I need to be able to do to maintain my own stimulation and the audience's?"

Asked if she's burning out:

"No, I don't feel that—I feel that, for as long as I feel that I am being effective, that I'm reaching people's lives in a way that lifts them up—I think that really one of my callings in life is to lift—lift people up."

Oprah agreed to a two-year extension of her show. Bob Iger of Capital Cities/ABC flew to Chicago to persuade her to stick with it and also to produce prime-time programming for other ABC divisions:

"I am looking forward to continuing with the show for at least another two years beyond this current tenth-anniversary season. It was a difficult and important decision for me personally because I wanted to feel completely confident that the show can still make a difference in people's lives and stay fresh and entertaining. It's never been clearer to me that the positive direction we're headed is the right way to go."

"I've wavered from week to week, from day to day. Two weeks ago my decision would have been completely different. Had King World not given the extension to October 6th [1995], I was going to say no. . . . Then I got a visit last Friday [September 29] from [Capital Cities/ABC president] Bob Iger. That really was the major, pivotal, deciding factor for me.

"Bob talked about the importance of the show to the ABC [owned and operated] stations and all that. But what he really did was offer me the support that would allow me to continue without being exhausted and overwhelmed. He also offered me long-range opportunities that will give me even more options than I have right now—in exchange for agreeing to continue for two years."

"One of the problems with me deciding whether I could continue was whether I could create the structure and the support system in order to do it. I felt that I was exhausted to a great extent, because we just don't have enough people . . . one of the things he offered was a support team—me having access to more of ABC's people and being able to use some of them.

"In my diary there's an entry from last Friday when I went home and I wrote, 'God, I've been looking for a sign, and today Bob Iger brought it.' It was relief to me. Like, now I see how it can be done. The sign was the opportunity to transition into the next phase of what I want to do with television. I'll have more to say about [the future] later."

"I have been encouraged by our loyal viewers to keep the show going, and I am thankful for the support of our affiliate stations across the country. This, coupled with other opportunities recently presented to me, helped me decide to keep on producing the show."

"The answer came from my gut. In the end I felt like it was best to go on and to continue to try to have a voice and say some things that needed to be said."

"There are moments, especially at the end of the season, when I'm tempted to quit because I'm tired. Every day can sometimes be a grind. It doesn't matter how spectacular the show is on Tuesday, you've still got Wednesday's coming up."

THE FUTURE OF HER SHOW

"I dream about creating. I haven't figured out what it is yet. But I dream about finding a new way of doing television that elevates us all. I really am tired of the crud. My goal for myself is to reach the highest level of humanity that is possible to me. That I have . . . that when I've done, when I've quit the planet this time around, hopefully last time, that I can say, 'Boy! I did that. Did I do it? Yes!' And I get up there and I high-five with the angels. High-five with them. And they say, 'Yes, girl. You did it.' "

1994

Asked how she'll deal with producing more shows:

"I'll deal with the prospect by creating more support for the team that I have. . . . When I tell people in the business that we have done this show for the past ten years with five producers, they laugh in my face. They say it cannot be done. It's an impossible thing. So this season we added five new producers. By the end of the year I'm going to double the staff."

1995

Asked if she would do an hour of shock to reattract lost viewers:

"I would absolutely quit first."

"ABC has made a commitment to *The Oprah Winfrey Show* until the year 2000, and I look forward to our expanded relationship and the creation of new programming. We have a long, productive history together, and Bob Iger has made it clear that our association will continue to mean that we can strive for the highest level in television. "

"I won't be doing this show ten years from now."

1993

"But the problem for me is not the show. I love doing the show. . . . But even knowing that, the problem is that I always just wanted work to be like a family. The mistakes that I've made over the years have come from that feeling, that if you're just fair and you're treated like a family, it'll be okay. Now

I realize it can't be done without infrastructure. You need systems. And you run yourself into the ground being the mother-sister-friend to everybody.

"In the end I felt like it was best to go on and to continue to try to have a voice and say some things that needed to be said. We're celebrating with champagne and no-fat pretzels. We're big-time."

"What we do will outlast all [the other talk shows]. Our intentions are much better. People see that, I'm telling you, they know the difference. They may choose to watch the spectacle for a while. But it will have a short life span."

"There will come a time, and the time is coming shortly, when I will make the shift. But for now the ratings are important because I've set myself up in this game."

1995

"I will do the show as long as it feels good to me. I'll quit if I do not think the work I'm doing is impacting people in a positive way.... For now doing the show feels good."

HER VISION FOR HER SHOW

"The last year has shown me I really can do anything. All the years I used to talk about how you need to create a vision for yourself and you can achieve it, that is really true. It was difficult at first because I was betrayed a couple of times. But the betrayal taught me that you can survive anything. All the things you thought you couldn't handle, you can."

1995

"I'm using my television show as a way of voicing my vision of what the world should be. What I do is lift people up with me, bring people to where I am.

"Life is all about evolving. . . . I'm very pleased with the way my life is progressing."

The Emmy Awards (and Others)

In 1990 she hosted *The Daytime Emmy Awards*. She explained the show as
     "The show with more tears than a soap, more prizes than a game show, more thanks than a prayer meeting, and more people with more things to say about other people than even *The Oprah Winfrey Show*."

On accepting her third consecutive Emmy for Outstanding Talk Show Host at *The Daytime Emmy Awards*, May 25, 1994:
     "Thank you very much. I tell you. Thank you again. It is. . . . This is getting to be nice. It is really a blessing and a real reward to receive this award for being able to be myself every day on the air. I really am. I feel blessed to be able to ask the questions that so many of you would ask if you had the opportunity to have the microphone."

At the 1995 Emmy Awards:
     "This is so sweet. It's truly a blessing to have this reward for doing something I so love every day."

OTHER AWARDS

On the occasion of receiving the *Ladies' Home Journal* One Smart Lady Award, February 1995:

"If you heed all of life's lessons, by the time you get to this age, you should have learned a few things. And I think I've learned a few things, but there are days when I don't think I'm very smart at all. That's why I am glad to have the award, so I can pull it out and say, 'But they said I was One Smart Lady, so why am I in this situation?' "

"It's what the Good Witch told Dorothy in *The Wizard of Oz*. 'It was always there. You always had the power inside.' And now that I'm forty, I recognize I always had it too."

Still, Oprah admitted:

"There are days when I've made the same mistake fourteen times, and I say, 'Do I have any sense?' Now I have an award to prove that I do. So every time I'm in the mistake pit, I am going to say, 'One day I was One Smart Lady—and I had four hundred witnesses.' "

"Oprahisms"

In 1971, radio station WVOL sponsored seventeen-year-old Oprah in the Miss Fire Prevention contest. She was the first black woman to win in Nashville. When it was down to three finalists, each was asked what she'd do if she had a million dollars. The first said she'd buy things for her parents, the second said she'd give it all to the poor. Oprah's answer:

"If I had a million dollars . . . I'd be a spending fool!"

Kicking off her shoes in the middle of a show:

"My feet are killing me."

1985

To porno film stars invited to appear on *A.M. Chicago* to discuss their work:

"Don't you ever get sore?"

"In terms of being very careful about what I say, I have decided to not be as much 'Oprah' as I can be when it comes to those kinds of shows, to think before I say things, because normally I don't. That's where 'Don't you get sore?' came from. I was just thinking, 'Oh, my God! This woman said, "Sometimes we work thirteen hours a day!" Well, how in the world do you do it?' "

On a 1987 show where a panel of rich bachelors were agreeing that they never expected to sleep with a woman on the first date, she turned to the slickest of them and said:

"How about you, Jimmy Jams? You don't look like you say, 'Let's wait.' "

To the audience:

"How many guys here have slept with a girl on the first date?"

To a female scientist on the show:

"If you had your choice, you'd like to have a big one if you could! Right? Bring one home to Mama!"

(Note: This one is always listed as a starred item in any collection of Oprahisms.)

When the Ku Klux Klan wives turned down her invitation to lunch, she responded with an unbelieving comment:

"Even if I *paid* for it?"

To Sally Field:

"Does Burt sleep with his toupee on or off?"

Sally replied, "I . . . beg . . . your . . . pardon."

In response to best-selling author Jackie Collins's remark "I think today women are looking for brains rather than brawn [in their heroes]":

"Yeah, but brawn's not bad. *Brawn's not bad*."

"I say minks were *born* to die!"

With Bob Wieland, a Vietnam veteran who completed a 2,784-mile Walk for Hunger:

"Weren't there some steps in the middle that were pretty hard? I mean, really, Bob! Right around Kansas? Goin' through all that hay . . . Gettin' all that hay stuck between your fingers. Wasn't that pretty hard?"

"If I'm not every woman, I definitely have been every size!"

1994

In response to a visiting sociologist who described a situation in which two female roommates who were just good friends suddenly evolved, virtually overnight, into a lesbian couple:

"I'm *never* getting a roommate!"

To actor Dudley Moore:

"Aren't there some technical problems posed by your habit of always wanting to sleep with taller women?"

In a serious discussion about television commercials, the talk turned to the kinds of commercials made for Calvin Klein clothes:

"I hate *all* those jean ads. They all have such tiny little butts in those ads!"

HARPO PRODUCTIONS

The Studio

"Home and studio are the only places I feel totally safe and secure. In my TV studio folks are like guests in my home."

1985

On obtaining ownership and control of her show and producing it through her own Harpo Productions:

"It was time for the transition. It puts me in the position to be in control of my time and my life. . . . Eventually I'm going to buy a studio and produce things for other people."

1988

In a 1987 *60 Minutes* interview Oprah commented on her almost all-white staff, saying that when the show expanded, she planned to hire more black people:

"I also believe in excellence, and the people that I have are excellent. I mean, it would be absolutely ridiculous to get rid of those people just because they're white, you know. That's racism in reverse. So as we bring on additional staff, you know, I will make sure that there's some black people included."

1987

In 1988, Harpo Productions, owned by Oprah, obtained ownership and control of *The Oprah Winfrey Show*. ABC stations would carry the show for five years, King World would distribute it. She bought the production facility in Chicago, which she renamed Harpo Studios. She invested an additional ten million dollars remodeling the studios:

"Had I not taken ownership of the show, I would not have pursued the whole idea of having my own studio. One thing would not have worked out without the other. I did this to really expand into the areas I wanted to and take over the show to create more time for me to do features and TV specials."

"When I first approached the idea of owning the show myself, it was really scary for me because I've been accustomed to a slave mentality."

1989

In August 1988 Oprah was saying that she wanted to cut down:

"I used to take every phone call from a guy who said he would jump off a building if I didn't talk to him. But I no longer feel compelled to aid every crazy. For two years I have done everything everyone asked me to do. I am now officially exhausted."

In 1990 she ran a VIP tour of Harpo Studios for thirty-one newspaper and magazine reporters:

"I don't want to sound like I'm patting myself on the back, but I think I have managed to handle all this very well because I have insisted on having control. Yes, I do have people to organize my life, but nobody organizes it without me knowing what I'm doing."

"It's no fun if somebody else does it. I picked every piece of tile, every doorknob, every gidget, every gadget, every carpet sample."

"It is absolutely the bread and butter, and I love that *Oprah Winfrey Show*. It is the foundation from which everything else has grown. It is the reason why there is a studio. It is the reason why we will be producing our first made-for-television movie this fall. It is the reason why I'll be able to take off next spring to shoot my own film. I never imagined that."

She spoke of the work of her studio:

"Yes, most of the things I have bought so far have been black written projects. I don't want to do exclusively black work. What I'm looking to do is work that means something.

"I need at least two other projects that are very different. I'd like to play a more contemporary role, something sexy—with my clothes on—something fun. One of the things people don't know about me is I'm really very funny."

1989

In March 1990 Harpo Studios opened, and *Brewster Place*, the series, began taping there:

"It's hard to put into my mind that this all belongs to me."

[91]

In 1990 she told opening-day visitors:

"We created this so that I would be able to do what I've told you before that I want to do. I just want to do good work, so I have created an environment for that."

Oprah is the first black to own a major studio facility, and the third woman (after Mary Pickford and Lucille Ball):

"Words can't really express how this feels. I was jogging yesterday when it finally hit me. I never think about how far I've come, but there are moments when I think, 'This really is something.' I think this is the 'big time' I've heard so much about."

"Right now I make a lot of money."

"You can only buy so many towels and so many houses. . . . Money is not the issue. The purpose of [Harpo Productions] is to invest in projects that we think are worthwhile."

"It is my greatest frustration that I have created a studio . . . and I can't star in movies because I don't have the time."

1995

Management Style

She inspires loyalty by treating people
"like I would want to be treated, and I allow them to make mistakes."

1993

"To me one of the most important things about being a good manager is to rule with a heart. You have to know the business, but you also have to know what's at the heart of the business, and that's the people. People matter."

1995

"You have to surround yourself with people you trust, and people that are good. But they also have to be people who will tell the emperor you have no clothes."

On the 1994 shakeup at Harpo Productions:
  "I made mistakes. My goal is to be fair."

Debra DiMaio

"I owe everything to her."

1986

She gave producer Debra DiMaio a six-carat diamond bracelet; the card read:
  "Brilliance deserves brilliance."

1987

"A lot of the producers had difficulty with the way Debbie dealt with them. And my only problem over the years with Debbie has been the way she dealt with people. I've done the show for so long with her, and she was my right hand and my left hand and part of my brain. So I just would not even imagine doing it without her."

1994

Debra DiMaio was characterized in a 1994 *TV Guide* article as "dictatorial and icy":

"Those are not words I would have chosen. Debbie was more of a taskmaster. I'm more willing to let a person make a mistake."

"She was a really good friend, a partner. She is the last person I ever thought wouldn't be here. I remember shortly after we had our conversation and she said she would resign, I'd have these flashes. I'd be driving down the street and I'd suddenly think, 'Oh, Debbie's gone.' It was like a death in the family."

On letting Debra DiMaio go:

"This is how you know you really have a friendship, if you can go through something like this."

From *Entertainment Weekly*, September 9, 1994, when asked, *The word is that [DiMaio] was too much of a dictator and the other producers couldn't deal with her:*

"Basically true. . . . I just didn't like the idea I heard that we were good cop–bad cop. I never wanted anyone to be the bad cop. She was intense, she was driven. My style is certainly more casual."

From *Ladies' Home Journal* November 1994:

"Now that I am [doing the show without DiMaio], I think, 'Oh, this is what I was supposed to be learning? Yes, the show is evolving, and now it is time for you to take complete control.' "

Asked about the complaints of her employees (in relation to Debra DiMaio) and whether she felt bad about driving them:

"No. Because as an adult you always have to take responsibility for your own choices, and everyone who is in this, I think, field of communication, be it news or a newspaper, any form of television or film production, understands the grind that it is, and it really is a grind, that it's preferable to your young, early-twenties, single years. It is not a grind that affords itself well to somebody who wants to have balance in their life. I feel that that's a choice that you made. You got paid very well for it. You were treated well. You were treated with honor and kindness and treated with a sense of dignity and that was the choice that you made for your career."

1995

She brought in former colleague Tim Bennett from WTVD in Raleigh-Durham to act as president of Harpo and promoted senior supervising producer Dianne Hudson to replace DiMaio as executive producer:

"One of the mistakes I made as a manager was assuming everybody could come up through the ranks. I always wanted to give the guy who carries the mail a chance to move up the ladder."

The Deal With Disney

In October 1995 Oprah and Harpo Productions entered into an exclusive long-term agreement with the Walt Disney Motion Pictures Group to produce motion pictures over the next five years:

"I've got a deal a minute, but now I don't have the time to deal with it."

"This is something that I've been wanting to do all my life. I'm aligning myself with a company that I have great respect for. I want to do family films. I will do adventure films. I will do historical drama. Anything that shows the possibilities of what a human being can do and the human spirit can achieve.

"I'm going to have to expand the production company. This is for my personal self. I'm going to devote my time after my shows to film projects."

"This is the fulfillment of a lifelong dream for me. I have wanted to make feature films since college. Being associated with Disney makes me ecstatic, because they share our passion for doing good work. We are looking forward to *Beloved* and are thrilled that Richard LaGravenese is going to adapt this incredible and powerful novel."

"I would rather do a film than take a vacation. This is the thing I've waited a lifetime for."

Looking to the Future

"When I look into the future, it's so bright it burns my eyes."

"I want to be working on projects that are meaningful. I know that can sound superficial. But it's true. I would like to be able to say, down the road, that I created a legacy, something even more enduring than anything I've done yet."

1993

From an interview in *Atlanta Journal*, October 30, 1995, when asked *So what's your future?*

"I'm just trying to do my little part and have a big voice and reach a lot of people. That's the power in TV—not in making the Forbes list of richest Americans, but being able to say something that gets people to listen and take action.

"I'm creating a prime-time series of specials for ABC that will be ready by the time my two-year contract ends. I also intend to do a series on race. Diane Sawyer and I have been talking about it for a year. Then the day after the O. J. Simpson verdict, I called her and said, 'Now's the time.' "

"But I'll never stop setting goals. My next one? I'm looking into biking across America in the summer of 1996. Just an idea. . . ."

From *TV Guide*, January 7–13, 1995:

"I'm really in a very different place now. I'm very pleased with the way that my life is progressing. I feel I'm finally, finally growing up."

From an America Online interview, October 3, 1995, when asked, *What do you see yourself doing ten years from now?*

"That's such a tough question for me. It shouldn't be, but it is. I live in the moment, so it's so hard for me to see next week. I won't be doing this show ten years from now. If I am, come drag my butt off! Thank you."

The *"Almost"* Autobiography

She had signed with publisher Alfred A. Knopf, Inc., to write her autobiography:

"I stood before that [American Booksellers Association] convention and said, 'This is going to be a book that really empowers people.' I felt I needed to say more.

"I wanted to offer some insight, some clarity, and some wisdom that might benefit other people."

"Writing my autobiography has been the best diet I've ever been on. Facing the pain and shame of my life, looking it right in the eye and putting it on paper, lifted a burden from my heart. I discovered I didn't need food to make me feel better—I felt good without it."

1993

"As I peeled away the layers of my life, I realized that all my craziness, all my pain and difficulties, stemmed from me not valuing myself."

1994

"I did not feel that the book was the true representative of my spirit. You could find out exactly when I was Little Miss Firecracker. But then it was like, so what? What does this mean? That part just wasn't there, and that's the most important thing in the world to me now, understanding why things are, not just that they are."

1993

"I'm thinking, really, what I would like for my legacy to be is not, you know, what I did, how many houses I had, how big was the studio, but what was my life able to do for other people. So, when I'm able to write that book—and also I felt that I was in the heart of a learning curve for myself. At the time, I was just starting to lose the weight and losing it for the right reason. And up until the time I started to write that book, I was thinking all those years that weight for me was just because I liked french fries, and not understanding that it really was all the years of my abuse, all the years of me not being willing to confront the truth, all the years of me wanting to be a pleaser. All of that should be involved in an autobiography about yourself."

1995

"It was really wonderfully written . . . great detail and all that, but *what did it all mean?*"

On canceling her autobiography:
    "That decision was, at the time, the hardest decision I ever made."

Re rumors that she pulled her book because Stedman objected:
    "But it's not true. It was like this: After the [ABA] convention I was at a press conference, and a reporter at a news conference asked me, 'Aren't you a little young to be doing an autobiography?' And I became very defensive. I was stumbling all over, saying, 'Well, you know. . . .' And I

was so glad there was a fire at the airport that night, so that that little newsclip never made it on the air. Because I had made a fool of myself. And I thought, 'Whoa, buddy. This is a sign.' "

Stedman pointed out that her memoir lacked introspection:

"Was a great detailed history enough? My experiences were meant to empower people and make sense of life."

She didn't want people to feel that Stedman had squelched the book:

"He didn't say anything was too explicit or shouldn't be said. He said it wasn't powerful enough. I prayed and cried . . . I feel bad about disappointing people. I went back on my word. But I finally said [to myself], 'Congratulations. You have always done what other people expected of you, and now you've done something for yourself.' "

From *Entertainment Weekly*, September 9, 1994, when asked where letting Debra DiMiao go rated on the emotional Richter scale of her life:

"The highest, the biggest, the toughest thing I've ever had to do. Before that it was canceling the book. I didn't want to disappoint Knopf or the coauthor. They had that party—I was actually looking for ways to pay them back for the shrimp! I think I've paid them back, though, with that Rosie book."

"It was an autobiography. It had all the details of my life right, but it didn't have any message. It didn't offer any hope about tomorrow, so I didn't think it wise at this time. There may be one somewhere, down the road, but not now."

In 1993 she spoke to Laura B. Randolph in *Ebony* about her autobiography:

"I wanted to write a book that would empower people. A book that would connect the dots of my life in such a way as to give it meaning and in the process offer some sense of wisdom for other people in their lives. But I didn't have the clarity or the insight yet where I thought I could do that."

"I did not feel that the book expressed a sense of empowerment for other people. I thought that it was really wonderfully written, in terms of the details of my life and in terms of how I had grown up and what had happened in my career, but I really wanted to write something that I felt was going to leave people with a message of great hope for themselves. And I'm not really prepared to write that book now because I'm still doing that for myself."

"I no longer think that an autobiography is what I should be doing. That is not how my life should be used."

"The best decision I ever made was not to write that book. I was in the heart of the learning curve, and I didn't know how deep that was. Even in the past year I've learned things about myself that I'm glad I didn't write in an autobiography."

"It's the hardest thing I've ever had to do. I knew everyone at Knopf would hate me, and, like I've been telling you, I hate to have people dislike me. But I also just knew this was right. The book just wasn't there yet. But working on it has been wonderful therapy. You know, I was going to name my abusers in the book, which I've never done. But then I realized, the very fact that I could consider doing that meant I wasn't scared of them anymore. They no longer had power over me. And that was enough. That set me free. At that point I realized I no longer *had* to publish the names. I was already free.

"It wasn't easy. It caused me a lot of soul-searching just putting their names on paper. But it was liberating."

Asked if she will ever publish the names in the eventual book:

"Maybe. Maybe not."

Will she publish the book at all?

"Absolutely."

ON TELEVISION

The Medium of Television

"This medium of television is so powerful and has the ability to empower people and affect lives in such a way that you really have to have the intention to do more than just not do harm. But the intention has to be to do some good. So, I changed the way I thought about television, and decided I was more than just a talk show host, even though that's what they call me. That it was indeed a way of being a voice to the world, a way of allowing whatever I felt and the people I surrounded myself with felt, to empower, uplift, enlighten, encourage, and if we can entertain you, we're glad to do that too."

On Monday, May 4, 1992, Oprah taped two shows from Los Angeles after the Rodney King verdict. The first almost turned into a riot when looters and victims confronted one another:

"I wasn't frightened of physical harm, because I recognized that people just wanted to be heard. Martin Luther King said that rioting is the voice of the unheard.

"It was stirring. It was what television should do. It was utilizing the power of media for the good. You can't do better than that, I think."

[103]

"Television is a reflection of who we are and who we say we want to be. It's time to offer new choices, new possibilities. It's time to elevate our potential."

"It's the best vehicle for change—even though it's often misused."

"The wonderful thing about this medium is that it allows people to know they're not alone. That's one of the greatest fears in life. Most people think in the midst of crises they're the only ones who have ever gone through it."

"We want to let people know that. That's the beauty of good television. Good television should inform and inspire as well as entertain. So much of television is simply mindless."

"I find what people say on television unusual, but it doesn't surprise me anymore. People have a *need* to tell someone, and the need overwhelms practicality."

"Management doesn't want problems, but they want ratings. I told them I'll be decent, and I was. They don't understand what women feel, and I do. Men think, for instance, that if you do a show about mastectomy, you can't show a breast. I say you *have* to show the breast."

1986

In 1995 Oprah Winfrey confronted the nation's broadcast news executives in a speech to the fiftieth annual convention of the Radio-Television News Directors Association in New Orleans and urged them to clean up their act:

"Let's abandon the 'if it bleeds, it leads' news philosophy of the past. Enough of the body bags, ballistic tests, and bizarre crime scenes. If you repeat a problem, the problem only gets repeated.

"We really ought to ask ourselves, Do we want our children to spend hours viewing the images we're putting on the tube these days? Do we want our children influenced by visions of death and destruction, carnage and car crashes, sex and scandals?

"Sure, we can ease our consciences by telling ourselves that all of this devastation and ugliness falls under the heading of news, of the public's right, need, and desire to know. But shouldn't we also ask this: What effect are these images having on our children, and do they really give today's youth a realistic picture of our world?"

"Stop focusing so exclusively on the negative, giving valuable national air time to the ugly, the dark the dysfunctional aspects of our society."

OLD-TIME TV

"I always felt better after watching *The Andy Griffith Show*, which, by the way, is still one of my all-time favorite shows. Life was so simple—the characters all really cared for each other, and the biggest scandal was whether those were really Aunt Bee's pickles in the pickle contest. Even though I never saw a black person in Mayberry, I always thought that if one of us dropped in, Andy and Aunt Bee would give us a slice of pie and make us feel right at home."

"It was a night that changed my life forever. Sunday night, December 27, 1964. The Supremes were on *The Ed Sullivan Show*. It was the first time I had seen a black woman on television with such beauty and grace. I was a ten-year-old girl sitting on a cold linoleum floor in Milwaukee. I was inspired by the possibilities of what I would be. That to me is one of television's greatest functions: to inspire us, to give us hope, and to help us improve our lives."

She said to Jane Pauley:

"And I really have missed an entire era of television, because I stopped watching television the night Mary Tyler Moore went off the air. It was my social life. The big *M*—I wanted a big *O* to go near my refrigerator because Mary had the *M*."

Pauley: *Why Mary Tyler Moore?*

"Because she worked in the newsroom, and that's what I did."

Those Other Talk Shows

Asked if she feels responsible for creating the confrontational, exploitative TV format:

"No, I absolutely do not. What I feel is that just as Donahue created the path for me, I have created the path for a lot of other people. The reason why there are so many talk shows today is because people were specifically coming after the Oprah deal and looking for the bucks. But how each host has chosen to use their voice is not my responsibility."

"I think we did a really good job of pulling ourselves away from the 'trash pack' last year. And it is a trash pack out there. I'm still kind of surprised, shocked, and embarrassed by what I see on a lot of the other shows. I think you can do television that is entertaining and responsible—and that people will still watch.

"I will not take the heat for being the one that caused what has happened. I think what we spawned was the notion of going after the 'Oprah bucks.' People wanted the bucks, and [talk shows] were easy to do—without any intention of doing something responsible."

1995

Asked if she ever watches the competition:

"I've always said I never look behind me. But over Thanksgiving I did see a few of the other shows. And the word that came to my mind was *base*. If you want to make a spectacle of people's lives, fine. But I don't appreciate it. I don't think it's necessary."

1995

These days Oprah is holding back none of her contempt for what she says many of the talk shows have become: "crap." And she has reserved special scorn for what she describes as "the humiliation, the purposeful degradation of black people in particular" on daytime TV:

"I saw a show where there was an entire row of black men, and the caption beneath their names was 'Men Who Know They Are Dogs,' and there was not a white face among them. When I see producers bring on black people in such a way that they fulfill every negative stereotype we have ever seen or heard, I am embarrassed for us."

Even King World syndicators hasn't cleaned up *Rolonda*:

"We've had that talk with King World. But they're no different than any of the other syndicators. They're interested in putting on shows that are going to get a [ratings] number and get them bucks. That's the bottom line."

"I feel that some of the shows must implode. I believe that most people want what's best for themselves and their families and they'll get tired of the trash."

"I've been guilty of doing trash TV and not even thinking it was trash. I don't want to do it anymore. But for the past four years we've been leading the way for doing issues that change people's lives. So I'm irritated and frustrated at being lumped in with the other shows. I think I'm blamed for it all. There was an article on the 'Oprahization of America,' lumping me and O. J. going down the freeway in the same category. I'm thinking, 'What is he talking about?' "

On the state of other talk shows:
   "I've been in talk show denial."

"I am ashamed and I think—I don't believe in censorship—but there needs to be some kind of regulations, especially somebody was just telling me about somebody's show where they had thirteen-year-old girls talking about having sex with each other. That should not be allowed on television. I don't care, the Freedom of Speech did not include that."

On the frequent discussion of teen sex:

"I think the television producers have to share in the responsibility of what will happen to this generation if young men and women only see that on the airwaves."

"Of course I'm embarrassed by a lot of what's on daytime television these days. I rarely watch, but recently I was on the treadmill and I saw this unbelievable show about one-night stands and people offstage who participated, then came onstage to meet again. Incredible. I think we have more to do than that, more to offer than that."

"We were never as whacked as they are whacked now."

"People should not be surprised and humiliated on national television for the purpose of entertainment. I was ashamed of myself for creating the opportunity that allowed it to happen."

"The time has come for this genre of talk shows to move on from dysfunctional whining and complaining and blaming. We're all aware that we do have some problems and we need to work on them."

"I wonder, is this a sign that my time in TV has come and gone? Should I just get out of the business and let 'The Kissing Contest,' 'Men Who Are Dogs,' and 'Big Butt Contest' rule?"

THE "FAME THING"

Celebrity

At age sixteen she went to Los Angeles to speak at a church and saw the stars on Hollywood's Walk of Fame. She told her father:
"One day I'm going to put my star beside those other stars!"

She appeared on *60 Minutes* on December 14, 1986:
"Mike Wallace! Lordy be! Is there something the matter with my taxes?"

Asked if it's hard to have a personal life:
" 'Hard'? Make that 'impossible.' "

"Women, always black women, three to four hundred pounds, waddle up to me, rolling down the street and say, 'You know, people are always confusin' me for you.' I know when they're coming. I say, 'Here comes another woman who thinks she looks like me.' "

1987

The "Fame Thing"

Winfrey's fans are legion and vocal:

"I was walking down the street the other day, and a woman bus driver pulled her bus over, jumped off it, and ran down the street to shake my hand. The bus was full, and this was five o'clock traffic, but the passengers loved it. Everyone was clapping, and I said to myself, 'This is something! I must be a somebody!'"

Sometimes fans tend to take advantage:

"I was having dinner with Stedman at a restaurant recently, and a woman at a nearby table recognized me and came over to chat. Then she called her husband over, and they helped themselves to chairs. When the waiter came, they ordered some dessert. Guess who had to pick up the bill?"

1987

"The life I lead is very exciting. Girl, it's fun. I have a good time, I phone for a limousine. I call room service, they ask you what temperature you would like your tea. Good life."

1989

"People bring me gifts and leave them with my doorman—bread and cakes, pickles and things; stuff like that. I walk out the door and there's always a bus there, and everybody waves, and then they tell everybody, 'That's where Oprah lives.'"

"I was sitting reading a paper, waiting for the plane, when this woman who recognized me came up and stood up and stood with her face so close to me, I could have kissed her on the lips—all I had to do was pucker."

She spoke to the woman for a few minutes and then went back to reading. The woman's friend scolded her for being rude:

"What is expected of me? What do I owe people? I realized I had to come to terms with this celebritydom. I realized I can't walk around feeling miserable because I didn't embrace everybody in the airport. So I don't hug people anymore. It's always made me feel uncomfortable. That's growth. But it took a woman in an airport to make me feel really, really, really bad all the way to Miami to see it."

1989

In 1992 she spoke about how celebrities deal with fame:

"If you come to fame not understanding who you are, it will define who you are. It shouldn't change you. If you're a jerk, you just get to be a bigger jerk. What fame does is magnify who you are and puts that on a platter for the whole world to see."

"It happened to me in Cap Ferrat at one time. I thought it was because I was black or something. I walked in, it was the Hotel de Cap or something, and there are these Germans in there, and I walked in and everybody put their forks down, and they turned and they looked at me. And this was like—forty pounds ago. So I thought that, 'Gee, they're not used to looking at black people in here.' So I thought 'Well, I am going to let them.' You know what I did, to the whole room? I curtsied to them, and told them I was Princess Sheba from some island."

"People send me things, little dolls and dollettes. Someone made an Oprah doll. Yesterday I got some homemade jam—dietetic."

"The thing I remember is that all the women said if they met Donahue, they'd be in awe. But if they met me, they'd ask me out to dinner."

On the hype involved in her show going national:

"You know, there's walking up to the line. I've danced on the line, but *this*! *This* was absolutely *over* the line!

"I'm beginning to feel marketed, you know? I'm beginning to feel like I'm 'packaged realism.' Which doesn't make me feel too comfortable, because I just am what I am. I'll be glad once the show has started [its national run] and people can judge for themselves. The hype is more than I can handle. I feel like I have to be the Second Coming. And I'm not. I'm just Oprah. Plain old Oprah."

1986

"I don't see myself as an icon. I see myself as a person who heads down to Walgreen's to load up on Nivea lotion. That's me."

1993

Does the affection you get from your fans make up for what you didn't get in childhood?

"Makes up for it twenty-million-fold. I was in New York last week and I was crossing the street and a woman said, 'I want to tell you how much I appreciate your evolution. I appreciate the fact that you are open enough to let us see it, because when I see that you can do it, I feel I can.' I wanted to weep on the street 'cause I thought, 'You get it!' To me that's better than any award, it's better than . . . I don't know if it's better than a 13 rating, though. Yeah, I'll take that 13.2, yes I will!!"

1994

"Celebritydom is dangerous. Adoration is unhealthy, because most people cannot put it in perspective."

She refers to her public self as "the Oprah image, the Oprah experience, the Oprah thing."

She says she's one of the most normal people she knows:
"I'm so happy that I'm normal."

Asked about both the public's and the tabloids' fascination with her:
"I think I'm sort of amazed by it all myself, but I don't consider it to be like a lot because everybody knows my best friend and everybody knows what my dog's name is. I think people have a sense of what the heart of me is like, you know. I believe that the heart of every woman is the same and the thing that I think that hasn't really, that I feel the most graced with [in] my life, is that the heart of me really has not changed. I feel connected to the heart of every woman, and man too. But I only understand the female experience in this lifetime."

Oprah told *Entertainment Tonight*:
"People don't treat me like I'm a star, or a celebrity. They treat me like I'm one of them. People say to me, 'Wait here. I'm going to get a pencil,' unlike with stars, who they'll say to, you know, 'Excuse me, Mr. Peck? May I please have your autograph? With me, it's 'wait here.' "

She said to Larry King:

"I think the external part of my life, I mean, where I live and, you know, what I drive, and what kind of panty hose I wear and can afford, and that kind of stuff—but I really do know that none of that stuff, in the end, means anything. The one—the thing that I'm most proud of myself about is that I have acquired a lot of things, but not one of those things defines me. I feel that I am the same person I was when your daughter, Chaia, came out on the show twenty years ago. And I feel like I am that same person. All of the stuff I read—you know, I'll look at magazines or tabloids, and it's just—it feels like something outside of myself. It doesn't feel like me. It doesn't feel like the heart of who I am."

1995

On Fame

While visiting her father, Vernon Winfrey, in Nashville, at age twelve, she was paid five hundred dollars to speak at a church:

"I told my daddy then and there that I planned to be very famous."

About being what she is:

"It's a lot of fun. I can tell you that. It really is a *lot* of fun. It certainly is more *fun* than I thought it was going to be."

1986

"This whole celebrity fame thing is interesting. I'm the same person I always was. The only difference between being famous and not being famous is that people know who you are."

"It's a kick. A kick with a capital *K*. I love it."

"I believe your personality is formed at a very early age. Fame can magnify that personality, for good or bad, but it can't change it. So when people say to me, 'Don't change,' I'm thinking, To what? To who? Who else would I be?"

"You know, my theme for the show is "I'm Everywoman," because I think my life is more like other people's, in spite of all the fame that has come to me."

Asked on *The Ed Gordon Show*, May 30, 1995, if there's something she wants to address that she's rarely asked:

"I really would love to talk about the fame trip because I think that to me it's the most fascinating part of my life. I mean I feel like I'm sitting back looking at my life happening, because I feel like I am the same person I've always been. And the reason why you read Stedman, weight loss, gain, weight loss, gain some more, and so forth, will she get married, no the wedding's off, he dumped her, is because it really is the fame trip. It's the whole, I don't know, experience created by the media because that is what other people have projected onto me and also onto Stedman and I think, you know, people or the media or the perception is such that you've got to put people into some kind of category or some kind of box.

"Now, when I first started out, I was in the, you know, fat-black-woman box, and nobody could figure out how in the world I had gotten to Chicago being not thin, not blond, not white, nothing that fit the mold of what a talk show host or hostess was, and so since that time, since nobody could really figure that out, I've seen myself, I've seen myself, I remember the very first time I lost weight, pulling out that wagon of fat, and the *National Enquirer* had done a story, you know, Oprah lost the weight and how she lost the weight, and it turned out to be their biggest seller ever, like in the history of the *National Enquirer*.

"And I knew then that I was in trouble. Because they now had figured out that I can sell magazines. So the peace that I had as a 'known person,' I knew that was going to be over. And so it has nothing to do with the truth, that's what's so fascinating to me about it."

In 1992 she did four prime-time specials focusing on show business:
"I've always been terrified of meeting celebrities."

"It's fun and interesting to remove the fame shield from people and look at a part of their lives that's not normally exposed."

"I think once you remove that fame shield, you have just folks."

Celebrities

During a chat with actor James Coco, who boasted about losing one hundred pounds:
"See, God was looking out for you. Sometimes she does."

1984

The celebrity she'd most like to date:

"I'd give up my right leg—for a week—for a date with Robert DeNiro.

"I could take a few weeks of this lifetime and give it all up right now if I could do a movie with him!"

1985

To David Letterman:

"When I was in the middle of auditioning, screen testing, I said to Steven, Steven Spielberg, if I may drop a name, I said, 'Harpo is Oprah spelled backward. I think that's a sign.' "

"I'd marry Dudley Moore tomorrow! I don't know a whole lot of guys shorter than me, but I'd marry that Dudley Moore tomorrow. He's wonderful. He's so funny, just naturally funny. And sincere."

She had met Maria Shriver in her Baltimore days. When Shriver and Arnold Schwarzenegger were married, Oprah had planned to recite from memory Elizabeth Barrett Browning's "How Do I Love Thee?" but worried that she might blow a line. None other than Jacqueline Bouvier Kennedy Onassis advised her, "Why don't you just take it up and read it?"

"I figured if Jackie O. says I can read it, I'll read it." And she did.

Candice Bergen appeared on *A.M. Chicago*:

"I had read *Knock Wood* and I wanted to sit down and have a nice talk with Candice. I realize this is probably difficult to do on television and be insightful, because that doesn't play in the suburbs at nine in the morning."

The day of her appearance, Oprah was suffering from a bad case of the flu:

"I was not good with Candice Bergen. She was excellent. She is the definition of a class act if ever there was one. There were moments when my vision, it was like I was seeing double. My head hurt. My energy was off. I was not in sync. I was really, really off."

Even Oprah Winfrey, the queen of talk, admitted she was tongue-tied when she shook the hand of Japan's empress Michiko at the White House state dinner on June 13, 1995:

"I didn't know what to say. And it was one of the few times."

On Christie Brinkley:

"Why wasn't I born with a body like hers?"

"Who really cares about her acting career? I want to know about her relationship with Billy Joel."

Recalling a piece of furniture from Christie's home, Oprah adds:

"And where did she get that pink couch shown on her interview with Barbara Walters?"

To Larry King on *Larry King Live*, January 4, 1995:

"I love the fact that you love your daughter so much. I really do love that. Every time I talk to you, and in any conversation, wherever we are, wherever we meet, you always bring her up. I think that—I hope my dad does that about me."

The "Fame Thing"

On Paul McCartney:

"I was the biggest Beatles fan. I had all the posters up on the wall, just like everyone else did. So, I'll tell you the truth, when I heard I was going to interview Paul McCartney—I mean, for a week I was so worried about what I'd ask him. And I never think about what I'm going to ask—ever! The red light comes on and I say, 'Well, something has to happen here.' But with Paul McCartney it was like, 'What am I gonna say? What should the first question be?' 'Paul, when I was a kid growing up I had all the Beatles' posters on my wall. Every morning I'd go to the posters and I'd say, "Dear God, please let me meet Paul one day." I wanted to know, all that time were you thinking about me, too?' That's how the interview started, and we had a hoot of a time, just a hoot of a time. Paul McCartney didn't even count because I thought to myself, 'Oh my God! I finally met him! Now I can die in peace.' "

Meeting Tom Selleck, Oprah impulsively asked, as her very first question, "Did you know your eyes are the color of a crystal-blue sea?"

By the end of 1987 Oprah's show was listed among the top five shows in syndication and she finally felt she had really arrived as a star. During the Christmas holiday she had been invited to Aspen, Colorado, by Quincy Jones and found herself rubbing shoulders with Barbra Streisand, Jane Fonda, Don Johnson, and so on:

"I'm one of the most boring people you'd ever meet. This Aspen Christmas scene was unbelievable!

The "Fame Thing"

"You walk into a room and there's Barbra Streisand and Jane Fonda sitting on the floor. You try to be cool: 'Oh, hi, Barbra. Hi, Jane. Nice to see you.'

"One night Don Johnson was having a party. So Quincy said, 'Look, babe, come to Don's house.'

"We get up to Don's house and I see people being turned back because their name isn't on the guest list. I say, 'God, if you love me, please let my name be on this list.'

"I get out of the car and a guy goes, 'Oh, hi, Miss Winfrey—go on in.' I think, 'There is a God! I didn't have to be embarrassed and turned away.'

"[When he opens the door] Don goes, 'Hey, Oprah. Here's a margarita.' Like he was expecting me or something. I go, 'Oh, God, I can't believe it. This is Don Johnson. I have arrived!'"

To Boy George:

"What does your *mother* think when you go out?"

"She says she never thought she'd be proud to have a son dressed up like a transvestite."

She was outraged at tabloid stories that had her and Roseanne warring over Roseanne's weight after Roseanne appeared on her show:

"There wasn't one single thing they said that was true. The truth is I never saw Roseanne after the show and, for the record, I never sent her Optifast in the mail as the story maintained. I did send her six bottles of Cristal Champagne and six dozen roses as thanks for doing the show— and received a lovely note from her in return."

The "Fame Thing"

Introducing David Schwimmer, who plays Ross on *Friends*:

"Our next Friend, now, he's an Oprah show in itself. His wife done left him for another woman—we did that years ago—then turns up pregnant with his baby."

PRINCESS DIANA

"Princess Di is number one on my wish list for guests."

Although Barbara Walters was Oprah's idol and role model, she wants to beat her out and have the first live interview with Princess Diana:

"Getting the princess would be the highlight of my career. I have a great deal of respect for her because she has shown that she no longer wants to be a princess on a pedestal."

"Well, I think—what fascinates me about her, I think she's even more interesting now that she's now not married to—well, not—you know, the situation is what it is. Because she is the classic example of the woman who had everything. She—the princess, the crown, the castle, and was still, with all of that external stuff, not able to attain happiness. She's a classic example of how you have to work from inside yourself."

"She is Ms. Cinderella, and still had to come to terms with, who am I, really? What does all of that mean? I think she's a great example to women all over the world."

"My reason for wanting to interview her would be totally different than

yours, because I think that I speak to the masses of women, because—
women and men, but women more so because I am a woman and I identify with that. And I just think that so many women struggle with their
own identity, and women believe that if they get that glass slipper, they get
the prince, they get the house, everything is going to be okay. And she is
proof that it isn't."

Letters

"The thing about it is, you get a hundred letters from people who say
you're wonderful. And then you get the one. . . .

"If you go to open the letter, and there's no return address on the outside, bad sign. Bad! Don't open it. It'll ruin your day."

"I get all kinds of mail. You should see the mail. I still answer it. I hired
someone to help me, I can't do it all by myself anymore. And now she
needs someone to help her. We've gotten a new computer system that
keeps files and so forth, so that you don't have to write every letter over
every time. I hate those letters that sound like they were written seven
years ago and nobody's revised it since then. So I try to be personal in each
letter."

1986

"I see that the show has evolved and I get four thousand—an average of four thousand letters a week from people telling me what a difference the show has made in their lives."

1991

"Every one is more personal than the next. I mean, all of them are just incredibly, 'You're the last person I have to turn to' kind of letters. And yes, I suppose it's a responsibility, if you look at it that way. But we just look at it as another adjunct to the show. We don't do a show without offering [help] to people."

"So all the thousands of letters I get every week—I do—do get thousands—where people send me their Sears bill, their electric bill."

"Oh, yeah, absolutely. And then get really upset with me when they're not paid. They send you the late notices saying, 'You didn't pay it.' It's absolutely true."

"I started a monthly luncheon club for my hate viewers. I read all the mail and pick out twelve of the most hostile witches and I take them out to lunch. The first time, I spent four hours talking to them. We drank fourteen bottles of Champagne!"

The Tabloids

"The only thing I hate about the press is the tabloids. I think they're verbal pornography."

"I never talk to them, they just write whatever they want."

"I was in Marshall Field's, buying some things, and this woman says, 'Oooh, this must be for your bridal registry.' And I said, 'No, it is not. I just need some cups.' But guess what I read in the gossip columns?"

1993

"I know everybody's watching what I'm ordering to eat. I don't even have to think that.

"I know that somewhere they're in the bushes. And they take, just the worst shots. Ahh, when you're putting the food in your mouth."

1995

"There are times when some little obscure magazine or some little obscure gossip page will say some horrible things about you."

Re tabloid reports of her being pregnant:
  "If I'm pregnant, I don't know it."

Re tabloid reports she had plastic surgery:
  "I have not had any plastic surgery, and if I have some plastic surgery, I'd tell you about it. Did you see the one that said I wanted to run for president?"

"Stedman came in to me today saying he's upset because the same paper says that I bought him a roadster for thirty-five thousand dollars and he wants to know where is it?"

"I just—you know what I think? I think this, America. I think that when people can continuously print things about you that are not true—and I'm—I—you know, I live a life of a celebrity and all that stuff, and people always say, 'Oh, that just comes with the territory.' I think it's a very dangerous sign in America when it can continually happen again and again. Because today it's happening to me, in a couple of years it might be you."

FRIENDS AND MENTORS

"I don't make new friends easily. I made friends when I did the movie *The Color Purple*—like Quincy Jones—who have become lifelong friends. But I'm very wary. When someone says, 'Oh, my God, I can't believe it's you! Could you just go to lunch with me, let me touch you?' it scares me. It makes me feel that what I do is so high on a pedestal—so far removed from what you do—that we could never really have anything in common. Who wants to be adored? You want to be able to relate to a person woman-to-woman."

"People often ask what do you do when you go home. Well, lots of times I'm on the phone with my girlfriend, Gayle, and when I'm going for a wisdom check, I'm on the phone with Dr. Maya Angelou."

Asked who has been one of the greatest influences of her life:
"Maya Angelou. You know, when I grew up and I first read *I Know Why the Caged Bird Sings*, I thought she was talking about my own life. So I grew up reading and relating to books and authors and never imagined in my life—I have the most graced life, my God—that I would end up in a mother-daughter-sister-friend relationship with Maya Angelou. So she's had a tremendous impact on me.

"My fourth-grade teacher, Mrs. Duncan, because, for so many years I wanted to be a fourth-grade teacher, because what she did was not just [teach] me long division, but really, that's where I learned to love learning, in the fourth grade."

Gayle King Bumpus

In 1976 in Baltimore she met Gayle King Bumpus, who would become her best friend:

"Gayle and I met in 1976, in the newsroom of WJZ-TV. I was an anchorwoman, and Gayle was a production assistant. One night there was a terrible snowstorm, so I invited Gayle, who was then living about thirty-five miles away, to stay in my house. She did—and we sat up and talked until dawn! Ever since then we talk every day, sometimes three or four times!"

Oprah gives Gayle credit for supporting her move to Chicago:

"When I was offered a job with a talk show in Chicago, no one thought I would take it because the show was at the bottom of the ratings and it was up against *Donahue*. But Gayle said, 'Leave Baltimore! I *know* you can beat *Donahue*!' Gayle has always been supportive of me, and telling me to move to Chicago was the best advice she's ever given me."

"Gayle helps keep me grounded and centered. She adds balance to my life. We've been friends since 1976 and have a relationship like none other. We're like blood sisters."

1989

Jeffrey Jacobs

Speaking of her friend, lawyer, and partner Jeffrey Jacobs:

"He's the visionary. Most of what has happened is a product of Jeff's vision. Were it not for him, there's a very good chance that I would still be hosting a local show here in Chicago."

"He allowed me to see that not even the sky was the limit. I believe you could be anything within limits, and now I tend to believe you can be anything and you can really do anything."

Barbara Walters

"From the very first interview I did, I was imitating Barbara."

1992

Oprah later told Barbara Walters about the Miss Fire Prevention contest:

"I said I wanted to be a journalist because I was interested in having people understand the truth, so they could better understand themselves. And the judges asked, 'Well, what kind of journalist?' and I answered, 'Barbara Walters.' "

"The problem with most talk shows, I think, particularly local talk shows that you see around the country, is that everybody's pretending to be a talk show host. I first auditioned at nineteen for a job at WTBE and I had no idea what to do, so I pretended to be Barbara Walters. It seemed she was my only mentor. I used to watch the *Today* show, and I thought, 'I'll do what Barbara does.' I would sit like Barbara, or like I imagined Barbara to sit, and I'd look down at the script and up to the camera because I thought that's what you do, how you act, and you try to have as much eye contact as you can ... all from what I had seen Barbara do. That's why I'm so thankful to Barbara now. But the problem was that you can't pretend to be somebody else for too long. You need to develop your own sense of style. So sometimes I'd forget to be Barbara, and Oprah would start slipping through. I felt that that was certainly more comfortable for me, but in the beginning being Barbara was what saved me, because otherwise I'd be petrified. Now I don't pretend to be anybody but myself."

"I thank God for Barbara Walters. I think that without her none of us would be here. She's a pioneer and she paved the way for the rest of us."

She recalled an interview with Barbara Walters on *A.M. Chicago*:

"It was terrible, because I'm not really good with people that I like— not only like, but am enamored with! 'Finally I get to meet Barbara Walters!' I kept saying, 'Barbara, you're so pretty!' I mean, that's real objective. 'I love your pink sweater! Where'd you get your shoes?' "

Asked by Barbara herself who was the toughest interview, she answered, "Barbara Walters":

"Why? Barbara Walters was my mentor, Barbara is my idol! It's hard to interview people you really, *really* like, because you're *gaga*! You go through a period where—it's a Yiddish expression, 'kvelling'—you start kvelling and you say, 'Oh, I love you, and I love you so much, and I love you all the time, and I love your dress, and I love your beads, and I love your hair.' "

[At this point Barbara Walters interrupted her and added the obvious punchline: "—I just don't like *you*."]

Bill and Camille Cosby

"At one time I read everything anybody wrote, and I'd call to talk to critics when something hurt, to tell them I'm not a sleaze. But Bill Cosby told me there would come a time when it would not hurt, and then I would know that I was growing up. I'm at the point now where I feel like I'm not in it."

1989

On November 5, 1989, one year after she reached her lowest weight, she devoted her show to a discussion of her constant struggle to keep from gaining back the weight:

"I went over to Mr. Cosby's house to have some sweet potato pie. He then said, 'This really isn't the best sweet potato pie. I have some really good sweet potato pie.' And he sent three sweet potato pies to my hotel, which I continued to eat for the rest of the week. . . . You know what happens once you get off course."

"Turning forty has been major for me. Camille Cosby told me it would be. She said 'There will come a time between forty and forty-two when you

[131]

will really have tired of other people's stuff. You will get very clear about what it is you really want to do and you won't care what other people think.' And it happened. I don't know exactly when or why. Camille said it is the realization that time is really all that you have, and when you reach forty, you will not be as willing to let other people use and abuse yours."

1995

Following advice from Bill Cosby, Oprah signs all the checks:

"I think not signing the checks and not knowing where the money is, is a sign that you are losing control. It's God's way of telling you that you have too much."

Maya Angelou

After sharing her great shame (about her drug use in her twenties) with her mentor, poet-author-actress Maya Angelou, Winfrey said she was bolstered by her comforting response:

"I shared this with Maya Angelou . . . and you know what she said to me? It really turned my life around, and I say this to you, 'You did then what you knew how to do, and when you knew better, you did better.' And I'll never forget that."

"Nobody makes it alone . . . and that's what Maya has been, a mentor and inspiration in my life. Everybody who gets through the tough times gets through the tough times because there is somebody standing in the gap to close it for you."

On presenting the NAACP's Spingarn Medal to Maya Angelou:

"Her words move me. Her words gave voice to my feelings. . . . She teaches us to strive. She gives me inspiration and clarity. Most important, she told me to be bodacious with my courage. All that and she can cook, especially smothered chicken and rice."

1994

Quincy Jones

Quincy Jones had seen her show while in Chicago and knew she was the right person for the role of Sofia in *The Color Purple*. She called the day she heard she had the part:

"the single happiest day in my life."

"Quincy is the first person I have unconditionally loved in my whole life. He walks in the light. If something were to happen to Quincy Jones, I would weep for the rest of my life."

OPRAH WINFREY, ACTRESS

On Acting

"When I was a little girl in Mississippi, I never even saw a television, and growing up in Milwaukee and Mississippi and Nashville the thought never occurred to me to be on television or to be the host of a show. I wanted to be an actress."

Asked if she's an actress or an interviewer:
   "Both, with a difference. I'm a good interviewer largely because I taught myself how. But I was born to act."

"I have been an actress in spirit all my life, and knew that was what I was born to do. I feel very blessed that I was discovered by Quincy Jones and that he also had this vision to know that I could do it."

"I'm a great mimic. I'll ride with a cab driver who speaks Spanish and I'll start talking with a Spanish accent. That's why I make it a practice never to watch Phil Donahue. I'm afraid I'll begin to look like him."

"I remember in high school, when I was competing in drama, I used to do matriarchal figures all the time, Sojourner Truth and Harriet Tubman, characters like that. So it's just a crossover. I believe everything you do in your life prepares you for the moment which you're living now. So it makes sense that I would be doing this."

"You cheat your ego. You know, in normal life you get up in the morning, you tell yourself who you are. You're ugly. You're smart. You're powerless. And then you go out and behave as if that's what you are. When you're acting a part, you just tell yourself something else."

"I'm going to continue acting. I think it's very important. And you will only see me do roles that I consider important. I'm lucky enough to be in a position not to have to act to pay the rent; and so I can choose good work and develop good work for myself."

Her first acting job was on TV on the ABC soap opera *All My Children*. Creator Agnes Nixon had appeared on her Baltimore show, *People Are Talking*, and Oprah confessed that she was a fan of the show. Later she was asked to appear in a small part on the show:

"I'm so blessed!" Oprah told Luther Young of the *Baltimore Sun*. "Imagine *me* doing this. I'm trying not to be excited—I'm trying not to be starstruck."

Oprah's scene (with Kathleen Khami) took place in a restaurant named Nexus:

"I can't believe I'm in Nexus without a date. It's just like in Baltimore.

"I always thought people in the background were just mumbling. These fools were actually asking me about the weather.

"Someday I'd really love to do this. I'm just a show-biz kid."

"One thing I learned from doing *There Are No Children Here* is that I don't want to be an actor full-time—even though, for a while, that's what I was saying I wanted to do. But it's hard work. And the great parts, the ones that make you say, 'I *have* to have that part,' don't come along very often. I would like to star in *Beloved* [the book by Toni Morrison], but I'm going to make myself read for it. If I'm not the best actress, someone else will star."

1993

Oprah told *Entertainment Tonight*:

"It's that much more enjoyable to me when people say, 'I've gone to that movie and I forgot it was you'—meaning me, Oprah Winfrey. I think, 'God, I did it! I did it!' "

Her Career in Movies

"You can sit around and wait for others to do it for you, but that way you get offered schlock scripts. When I find good work, I try to purchase it and see that it gets done. I don't have to be in all of them. I'm just interested in seeing good work come to the screen."

Oprah Winfrey, Actress

Oprah revealed on *Entertainment Tonight* that she was ready to play a role of a woman who understands her sexuality:

"I keep playing all these old women with gray hair and stockings rolled up on their legs. I'm ready to cut loose, let loose, and let it go!"

She announced that she wanted to do more movies and still continue with her TV talk show:

"I intend to do and have it all. I want to have a movie career, a television career, a talk show career. I will continue to be fulfilled doing all of these things, because no one can tell me how to live my life. I believe in my own possibilities, and I feel I can do it all."

"Having a talk show is a great position to be in because it means that I don't have to make movies to make money and pay bills, and I can choose only the best work. I'm interested in doing roles, creating lives on screen, on film, that in some way help people to better understand themselves and see a bit of glory in other people."

Asked about future movie plans:

"My problem is not enough time, not enough good scripts. I won't play a character who shoots or is shot at, who's raped or stalked or battered. That leaves me with a limited number of roles. I keep waiting."

Movie roles she'd like to play:

"Madam C. J. Walker, one of the first black female millionaires—she invented the straightening comb."

"I'd like to do Dinah Washington—a great, great blues singer who had several different husbands and used to sexually exhaust her men."

THE COLOR PURPLE

"This summer I've just finished reading Alice Walker's *The Color Purple*. I read a review of it in *Newsweek* and bought it the same day. It's very different. It's a series of letters written in novel form. I liked it a lot."

She told Lou Cedrone of the *Baltimore Evening Sun:*
   "If you got married, you got a copy. If you had a baby, you got a copy. If you divorced, you got a copy. I thought it one of the best books I had ever read."

She said she thought:
   "Oh, my God! I'm not alone. I was sexually abused as a child, and when I read about Celie, I couldn't stop. I wrote my own 'Dear God' letters [as Celie does], and I identified with all those people. There's magic in that book."

In 1984 Steven Spielberg cast Oprah in *The Color Purple*. She has said that when she heard about the movie, she prayed:
   "I prayed at night, 'Dear God, find me a way to get into this movie! I would have done anything, best boy, or water girl."

She told Nan Robertson of the *New York Times*:
   "After I read this amazing book, I sat down and wrote to Alice Walker,

with a résumé and all my reviews and references, telling her I would go anywhere to audition if this was made into a movie."

It was a stroke of luck that Quincy Jones, passing through Chicago, turned on Oprah's show and thought she was the right person to play Sofia:

"There was a message left that Reuben Cannon had called about some movie, and I knew, I just knew, that it was *The Color Purple*."

Jeffrey Jacobs insisted Oprah get star terms for *The Color Purple*:

"I love getting paid, but I'd do this [the talk show] for free if I had to. When Jeff was negotiating for me to appear in *The Color Purple*, he was pushing, pushing. I said, 'Jeff, I'd do it for nothing—please, *please* don't ask for any more money!' He said, 'You're *not* doing it for free.' "

Oprah told Gary Ballard of *Drama-Logue*:

"The greatest moment of my life was when Steven [Spielberg] told Willard and me we had the parts. The [Oscar] nomination was not even as great. Maybe the day I was born was greater, but I can't remember that experience.

"To be cast in *The Color Purple* and not talk about it? I was giving some lectures around Chicago at the time to groups of about a thousand people. I'd say, 'I'm not supposed to talk about this, but . . . Now, don't tell anybody I told you.' I couldn't keep something like that to myself."

Appearing on *Late Night With David Letterman*, Oprah talked about that first encounter:

"First of all, you walk into a room and there is Steven Spielberg. It's pretty intimidating, you know. So the first impression is, 'Oh, my God, he's much shorter than I thought he was.' And then once you get over that, it's like, 'Oh! He said my name!' And I wanted to remember everything in the room, so that I could at least tell my friends and remember the moment!"

Although she'd been losing weight on a diet, she stopped dieting to play Sofia:

"They called me and said, 'You can't lose weight. Whatever you've lost, you'd better go out and find it.' "

Oprah told Stephen Hunter of the *Baltimore Sun*:

"I'm convinced that if I had sought *The Color Purple* and called Steven Spielberg and Quincy Jones and said, 'Listen, I really am a wonderful person, give me a chance,' it wouldn't have happened."

"I had Fannie Lou Hamer in the back of my head [referring to the rural Mississippi civil rights leader of the 1960s]. I thought of her being in and out of jail, so brutalized. I'm aware of my legacy, which is why I was honored to play Sofia. She was part of all those women I'd been carrying around inside me for years. In high school oratory contests, while everybody else did a speech from *Inherit the Wind*, I'd be doing something from Margaret Walker's *Jubilee*, about a slave woman after the Civil War, or Sojourner Truth's 'Ain't I a Woman?' speech."

"For the first time in my life I thought, 'What if I do my best and it's just not good enough?' "

"My first day, our first setup, the scene was mine. So I thought, 'I wish I had a day or two to see what they do.' I was quite intimidated."

Actor (and Oscar nominee for *A Soldier's Story*) Adolph Caesar played "Mister's" father:

"He told me to give myself over to the character and let the character take control. He told me to pretend the character had a life beyond the screen."

Of Steven Spielberg:

"He was intensely sensitive to every character. He knew what your character had for breakfast five years ago. He knew how she moved her eyes and how she would be feeling at any given moment and so how she would react."

"When Sofia makes her first appearance, she is walking three or four feet ahead of her husband-to-be, Harpo, to meet his father for the first time. The walk Steven gave me to do was quite powerful, very full of herself. And as I was walking, Steven said, 'Now, I want you to turn around and give Harpo a big smile!' Well, let me tell you, that smile made all the difference between a Trojan woman walking up the road and a woman who's quite sure of herself and kinda kidding around with her man. It made all the difference in the world."

She told David Letterman:

"What I would do when I had to cry is start crying early in the morning, so that I would make sure by the time I had to cry, I'd still be crying. I used to cry all day. I did."

Throughout the filming of *The Color Purple* she felt director Spielberg was cold to her:

"I thought, 'He doesn't like me, I'm going to get kicked off the set.' "

Actually he was engaging in a directing technique. At the premiere he told her, 'I realized how terrified you were, and that was working for you. That's why I never gave you any reassurance.'

"Everyone on the set, from the grip and the gaffer to Spielberg and the star [Whoopi Goldberg], gave me positive energy."

Curious about Spielberg, David Letterman jokingly asked, *Did you ever have any trouble with the guy?*
    "No trouble at all.
    "We were doing the 'Juke Joint' scene. Steven came over to me before the scene and asked if I could cry. You know, Steven Spielberg asks you to cry and you want to give him buckets of tears.
    "He wants a tear falling out of that left eye so when you turn to the camera it's falling right there. And I couldn't. I was so afraid that I was not going to be able to cry, I started plucking out my lashes and sticking them into my contact lens, and still could not cry."

Oprah said she tried to think about all the horrible things that had happened in her life and still she couldn't cry.

"When I saw I wasn't going to cry, I prayed for death right then and there. Steven said it was okay. We'd do a second take. [By the second take, Oprah was still unable to cry.] I thought, 'I'm gonna go down in history as the actress who couldn't cry in a Spielberg movie.' He didn't seem upset, but said we'd get it another day. I left the set and cried all afternoon because I couldn't cry for him."

Oprah's most important scene is at the end of the film. As Sofia she is at the family dinner table after release from prison:

"Mine was the last angle to be shot. I had been sitting there watching everybody else. I had a lot of time to think about the years Sofia spent in jail and how thousands of men and women, all the people who marched in Selma, were thrown in jail and what those years must have been like. Sofia finally speaking was a victory for all of us and for me.

"She represents a legacy of black women and the bridges that I've crossed over to get where I am. She's a combination to me of Sojourner Truth and Harriet Tubman and Fannie Lou Hamer and grandmothers and aunts of mine and other black women who have gone unnamed but who represent a significant part of our history."

"It was a major breakthrough for me.... It was the day I became an actress."

Oprah told Lou Cedrone of the *Baltimore Evening Sun*:

"Spielberg said he couldn't include every incident, and that if he had, the film would've been too depressing. As it is, it's a joyous picture, a triumphant one. The essence and spirit of the book are there, and that's most important."

"I identified so strongly with the characters. I came from a broken home; I've seen so many Celies and Sofias in my life. I've known all these women."

"I'm a person who lives my life with great passion, and I think that comes across on camera."

Oprah Winfrey, Actress

Oprah retorted to criticism of the film at a special preview of the picture in Washington, D.C.:

"This is not a 'black film.' It's about endurance, survival, faith, and ultimate triumph. Whatever you want is in you.

"That's what we should be talking about. If this film is going to raise some issues, I'm tired of hearing about what it's doing to the black men. Let's talk about the issues of wife abuse, violence against women, sexual abuse of children in the home.

"What the book did for me, and what the movie is doing for other women who are sexually abused, is pointing up that you're not the only one.

"Every time there is a play or movie with white people in it, they don't expect them to represent the history or culture of the race. We aren't trying to depict the history of black people. It's one woman's story, that's all.

"I was surprised to see the way people reacted to *The Color Purple*. I believe people see what they want to see in a work of art. When you see joy and beauty in something, it's because it's a part of you. When you see negativity, anger, and fear in something, it's because it is a part of you.

"I tell people that the movie was not for or against men. It's egotistical and macho for men to even think it's about them. *The Color Purple* is a novel about women.

"Sofia teaches us that there is a great will and power inside us all, and that you can overcome anything. You can be down, you can even be broken, but there's always a way to mend."

Filming *The Color Purple*, Oprah later told her audience,

"was the one time in my life I experienced total harmony."

Oprah Winfrey, Actress

Oprah told Corrine F. Hammett:

"I was really depressed when we finished, because it was the best experience I ever had in my life and I felt never in my life will I be able to top those feelings."

"It was a spiritual involvement. I learned to love people doing that film."

Some people accused Oprah of playing an "Aunt Jemima" role:

"At first I was very kind. Now I'm just ready to slap them."

"Everybody was a joy to work with. We were a family."

NATIVE SON

Her 1986 film *Native Son* got mixed reviews:

"Nothing could ever beat *The Color Purple* for me."

She told David Brenner on *Nightlife*:

"When we were Negroes, we had to read this. It was required reading because it was a black book. He commits a crime and then his mother has to beg for his life. I think the essence of it is that we, society, create our own killers, our own menaces to the public, if we don't take responsibility, not only for ourselves, but for everybody else."

Winfrey patterned her role in *Native Son* after her mother, and she says one of her lines in the film particularly reflects her mother's helplessness:

"I did all I know how . . . and if I left anything undone, it's just 'cause I didn't know and 'cause I didn't see.' "

"It was good, because the character I played was a weary woman—tired, honey. It was good to have that, so I didn't have to *stretch* to play the character. It was exhausting. I really researched the role, but I was so glad to get it over with."

She told Regis Philbin:

"It's a very small role. Do not park your car if you intend to see me in this movie."

She told Rick DuBrow of the *Los Angeles Times*:

"It's one of those times when a little voice tells me, 'Shut up.' "

After a few short weeks, due to poor office box response, *Native Son* was quietly pulled from theaters.

THE WOMEN OF BREWSTER PLACE

On Gloria Naylor's 1982 National Book Award-winning novel, *The Women of Brewster Place*:

"The book makes a great statement for maintaining your dignity in a world that tries to strip you of it."

"I read a lot and I try to read as many black authors as I can. I was reading *Brewster Place* while filming *The Color Purple*, and I decided then that I wanted it to be [a filmed project] that I could take part in."

"It's a great story. It involves all these women and their spirit of survival."

The Women of Brewster Place was hard to sell to the white men who ran the networks. Initially all turned it down. Oprah recalled:

"They said it was too womanish. I said, 'Look, I know you are very wise and perceptive men and the only reason you have turned down this project is because you haven't read the book. You could not read it and turn it down. I'll be calling by Tuesday to see who's read it.' Only one wise, perceptive executive had read the book by the deadline, but he was sold."

"I was relentless. I'd call and ask, 'Are you reading it? What page are you on?' "

Re the controversy over *Brewster Place*:

"I believe that it is necessary to not be restricted in your work based on your color, and as long as you tell the truth in your work and your art, people have no right to tell you how to do it." She insisted that the production was "very concerned about the image of black men and took great care to try to help understand why they were that way."

"I just don't think you can allow yourself to be controlled. I'm insulted, too. I am more conscious of my legacy as a black person than anybody. I have a responsibility, not only as a black woman but as a human being to do good work. I am just as concerned about the images of black men as anybody, but there are black men who abuse their families, and there are white men who do it, too, and brown men. It's just a fact of life. I deal with it every day. So I refuse to be controlled by other people's ideas and ideals of what I should do."

"People said *The Color Purple* was a fluke for me. I had my own personal doubts. I discovered I really am an actress. If you have lived as a black person in America, you know all those women. They're your aunts, your mother, your cousins, your nieces."

When she saw the final cut of *The Women of Brewster Place*, she was thrilled:

"I am very, very proud of it. It was an incredible experience. I haven't done a lot of acting and I really enjoyed it. I love women, and working with these women was wonderful, because they're all so wonderful."

The miniseries aired in March 1989, one of the highest rated miniseries of the 1988–89 season. There were complaints about its portrayal (or lack) of black men. Oprah responded:

"The book is not untruthful about the portrayal of men. If it's not exploitative but it's truthful, that's what's important to me. For anyone to put me in that defensive mode makes me ill."

All the women on *Brewster Place* became friends:

"That's why our scenes work so wonderfully, because we've become really bonded here. Women have traditionally been viewed as being catty about each other, but there's none of that here. There's such a great spirit of . . . *womanness*."

Oprah was not nuts about her appearance in the miniseries:

"I can't believe I was that big, really. I looked at all the pictures of me that were taken only a few months ago, and I just can't believe it. I do believe in padding now."

"This is only the fourth time I've acted. I guess I'm a natural, but I'm very short on technique. I actually live the moment, almost like channeling the character. But once I release it, it's released. By the end of the day, when it's time for the closeup, I'm just emotionally whipped. Unless I can actually feel the pain, I think I didn't do it right. But you can't feel it for twelve takes."

1990

"Years from now this film will be remembered."

"*Brewster Place* is as important as anything I've ever done. I'd say I'm not putting my career on the line, but I'm certainly putting a lot of my professional expertise on the line. Because I'm not only an actress doing it, but I've said to the network, 'I *guarantee* you that this is going to work.'"

"Playing Mattie is a vacation from all the stuff that Oprah Winfrey has to deal with. Mattie's not in the *Enquirer*. Mattie doesn't have two hundred checks on her desk to sign. She's not running a studio. She doesn't have the whole celebrity deal."

"No one can deny that there are men—of all colors—like the ones portrayed in Gloria Naylor's book. But that's just one story. There are many other stories to be told."

She explained how she prepared for a role:

"What I do for all my characters is develop a little history book for them. So for me, it's almost like channeling; you just let the character take over."

"Most people out there have no contact with black people ever. Their only images are the ones portrayed on television.... There's a whole reality outside of what most people know, where the black community functions on its own, where people own businesses, where people care about their property and their children and pay their taxes. The point of having your own company is that you can show that."

She shoots a scene with a run in her stocking:

"It happened this morning in the unemployment office scene, and I decided to leave it on because Mattie would have a run. But I deliberately put on fat cotton underpants when I play her. It makes me feel like her."

She was fifty pounds heavier when she did the TV movie, and speaks about the struggle with weight:

"Nobody will ever understand what a struggle it is. There's something in my head that feels that Mattie should be bigger. The weight is a shell for her. It's hard, in my mind, to get rid of the shell and still feel comfortable with her. Because that's all that weight is anyway. It's a shell for protection. You act like Miss Stable because you feel you can't do anything else. You think you can't put on a red dress with sequins, so you might as well put on a housecoat."

On doing the *Brewster Place* series as well as her own show:

"We've fine-tuned things with our *Oprah* show producers. And in the acting I'm really a very quick study."

Unlike the miniseries, which was true to the novel, the series was much more Oprah's creation:

"We didn't try to change the movie, because that's what Gloria Naylor wrote. Now we have the opportunity to use what she wrote as just the root of all the other things that can happen."

Speaking of her character, Mattie, in the *Brewster Place* series:
"She had the 'Nobody Knows the Trouble I've Seen' syndrome. I've known women like Mattie all my life, I sort of carry them around with me. But they're not fun to play, and they're not interesting."

In the new series Mattie will be modernized:
"Otherwise she would be the downtrodden mother of the block, and there'd be nowhere for her to grow."

"I have no fears about this. What most people in television don't realize is that you don't have to fake real life. You don't have to have canned laughter or canned situations."

She worried about having taken on too much, what with the talk show and the *Brewster Place* series:
"It's going to be hard, and it will take a lot of time. I don't know how I will do it—but you do what you gotta do."

She softened the original story:
"How can we do a story about black people with no drugs or violence? The truth is most black middle-class and lower-middle-class people live like the people on *Brewster Place*. You work, have a sense of ethics, want the best for your children, and try to do what's right.

"I'm very hopeful, but if it doesn't work, I won't have the if-I'd-onlys, not at all. First *The Oprah Winfrey Show* is still my bosom, my root, and my foundation. Without it nothing else could happen. And I believe that when we finish our thirteen episodes, I can say I gave it everything, and that will be the truth."

The Women of Brewster Place was canceled after four episodes:
"I could hear my inner voice telling me it wasn't time, don't do it. My mistake was I didn't listen to the voice. And the voice—by which I mean the voice of God—was speaking loud and clear and I didn't take heed."

"Wasn't the time and I wasn't willing to listen to the instinct that said, 'Wait.' I should have waited. I was anxious."

SCARED SILENT

Arnold Shapiro had produced a successful TV program in 1979 featuring criminals who talked to teens about the horrors of prison. It was called *Scared Straight*. In 1992 he created a new program about child abuse, *Scared Silent*, and brought it to Oprah for her backing and involvement as narrator. She introduced the documentary:
"I'm Oprah Winfrey, and like millions of other Americans I'm a survivor of child abuse. I was only nine years old when I was raped by my nineteen-year-old cousin. He was the first of three family members to sexually molest me."

"You lose your childhood when you've been abused. My heart goes out to those children who are abused at home and have no one to turn to."

She spoke on *This Morning* (CBS) on September 4, 1992:

"I think this is a great move forward... Arnold Shapiro, who approached me to host the special, had already committed CBS—thank you—and NBC. PBS and I went to ABC—the head of ABC—and asked that—that they join in. So, at first I was pretty upset that they all—that ABC wasn't airing it at the same time as everybody else, but I think knowing that people who do miss it tonight—although I hope you won't miss it tonight—can watch it on ABC on Sunday—has been the positive side of all of this.

"I think it's really important television. It's one of the things I am most proud of. When Arnold Shapiro wrote me and asked that I be a part of it, before I finished the letter, I said yes. It was a resounding—no matter how much time this takes, I want to be a part of it. And I think people's lives will be powerfully impacted by watching. I think that's what television should do."

On *Good Morning America*, September 4, 1992:

"I mean that's an incredible commitment for a program that is not, you know, a happy, fun program, but almost—the kind of program that you would normally find on PBS... to understand that this is important enough to overlook ratings, overlook revenues, and just get the message out and try to help as many people as we can."

"It has become a mission for me, I think, on the planet here to try to make a difference in the lives of children, to take the abuse that I suffered as a child, to move on, make peace with my own past, but to try to enlighten and encourage other people who've experienced it to do the same for themselves."

On *This Morning*:

"I want children to see it because I think it would be just another lie to not let children see it—allow children to see it, because children are being abused. You know, one of the problems for me when I was a kid, that caused such confusion and such shame, is that I was taught that nice girls didn't have sex. They didn't do that kind of thing. And, on the other hand, family members were having sex with me. And so if I had just known that it was happening to somebody else, I think that could have made a major difference in the way I handled and processed those years of abuse. So if I had children, I would allow my children to see it, because unfortunately you never know what might happen to your child or what—how your child might be approached.

"And the unfortunate thing, as we know, is that the people who have the most power in a child's life, or the most influence, are the ones who are most likely to do it. If I had been, as a child, approached by a stranger, no doubt I would have told. I would have run home screaming, telling everybody. But because every time I was sexually abused, it was by either a family friend or a family member, I never did, I was one of those people who was scared silent until my twenties."

"On the other end of the 800-number are some people who are working with Child Help who are in the business of helping you find, in your particular area, wherever you live, organizations that can help you. I think it's very important—if you are physically abusing a child, you are causing psychological or emotional abuse and certainly sexual abuse, that you do get help. I don't think this is one of those problems in the family that you can handle just because you say, 'Oh, yes, I saw the special and now I'm going to stop doing that.' For me I think the special is to make—the purpose is to make people aware of their own actions and the damage that those actions cause. I think too often in this country, people don't make the connection between abuse as a child and don't understand that a child who's abused will later either turn on himself or herself, or turn on us, turn on society. And so, to understand that that's why the prisons are filled and that's why there's so much crime in the streets and that's why there's—teenage pregnancies are at epidemic proportions. We've got to start changing the way we treat children. Unfortunately we treat children as though they are property and not like they're people."

She had some of the subjects on her talk show; among them was a woman who confronted the stepfather who abused her:

"Seeing her be able to do it was a powerful thing. Being on television has been my therapy. When you help other people, you get help."

On the *Today show*:

"I am thrilled about it. I think it is a move in the right direction for children of this country, and for all the survivors and even those people who are abusing children. I think that this special is going to make a great impact, Katie [Couric]. I think it goes beyond television, in that it does what I think television should do, uplift and encourage and enlighten whenever it can. I watched the special, and wept the first time, and it moved me. And you know, every time—being a victim of child abuse myself, every time I think, 'Okay, I'm over it, that's it, I've moved on,' I somehow manage to encounter some experience that brings the episodes, or those experiences, more clearly into focus for me. So this special was helpful even to me, and I think that I've overcome just about all of it at this point."

"Oh, everybody's vulnerable, that's the thing about this. And I want to emphasize again that the special's not just about children who are sexually abused or experienced that, it's physical and psychological abuse as well. And it knows no bounds. It is in every class, in every color. And so that's why I think it will be so impactful because, you see, the interesting thing to me is that you never see middle-class families dealing with it. Most people think that it—it just affects people in poverty, and we know that that's not true at all."

THERE ARE NO CHILDREN HERE

In November 1993 in *There Are No Children Here*, a true-life drama about black families in a Chicago public housing project, Oprah played a caring mother trying to hold her family together. It was filmed on location in the Henry Horner Project, which Oprah drove by every day on the way to work:

"It will really touch people, I hope. I chose to do it because I wanted to put a human face on the projects. It's not some monolithic place where poor folks live. For many people it's home, and they live there the best that they can. I want to remind other people of that."

"Yep, I spent my summer vacation in the projects."

During filming she returned to her trailer at four A.M. to take a nap during an all-night shoot, only to find seven slumbering youngsters from the Horner Homes:

"There were three on the sofa, all with a blanket over their heads so they looked like little ghosts. Three on the floor and one on the chair. So I sat on the steps of the trailer."

At a church near the Horner projects the pastor thanked Winfrey "for coming and bringing a little hope":

"I just wanted to weep when he said that, because I realized, looking into the faces of those children, that's exactly what we had done."

"Maybe just one or two lives will be affected by our doing this movie. Maybe one or two kids will get more of a chance because of it."

She donated her entire $500,000 salary to a scholarship fund for the children of the Henry Horner projects. ABC later matched that amount.

She talks about how her life

"will never be the same . . . I used to see these kids from the projects walking down the street and think, 'Oh, my God, is something going to happen?' Now I look to see if it's one of the kids I know. That's the difference."

During the filming she met a twelve-year-old boy and took him under her wing. She helped both his mother and his older brother get jobs, enrolled the boy in private school, got the mother into counseling, and the family has since moved out of the projects:

"Kalvin's mother called me the other day, and I was crying on the phone. Do I cry a lot or what? She said, 'I feel like I'm in the movies because when I come home from work, my kids say, "Mama, how was your day?" This is the first time I have something to say.' "

"You find people in the projects who have as much desire for fulfillment and enrichment—to be somebody—as anywhere else in the world. The lesson is that we really are all the same and it doesn't matter how you're packaged; the heart is always the same."

Oprah has also tendered the half-dozen or so children she became acquainted with ("my little friends") a tantalizing deal:

"If they get their grades up and make all *A*'s, I'm taking them to Disneyland."

BELOVED

"*Beloved* is my *Schindler's List*," said Winfrey, who has held on to film rights since 1987, when she "read the review, read the book in one day, called up Toni [Morrison], and bought the rights. I bought it before the Pulitzer and before Toni won the Nobel Laureate."

"*Beloved* is my passion. I held it since 1987, waiting on the right time to do it and the right writer to come along and help me to develop it."

"What I want to do in my film is to be able to say, 'Can we just have some black people buy tomatoes in the grocery store?' To show that we are a thinking, feeling people."

"This is the fulfillment of a lifelong dream for me."

The Academy Awards

The Color Purple was nominated for eleven Oscars, including a Best Supporting Actress nomination for Oprah. It didn't win anything.

When asked by Gary Ballard of *Drama-Logue* how it felt to be nominated, Oprah responded:

"Wondrous, of course, but it's hard to describe. I don't know how I feel about it. It makes it tougher next time out. What do you do to top it?"

"It was the worst night of my life. I could not go through the night pretending that it was okay that *Color Purple* did not win an Oscar. I was pissed and I was stunned, and I was also in the tightest dress I've ever been in. It was a nightmare. The day before the Oscars, the designer who made the dress had come to the Beverly Wilshire, where I was staying. I tried on the gown. Fine. He said he wanted to taper it at the knee, and to hem it. The next day he brings the dress back. Five minutes before I leave, I go to put the dress on—it will not go over my head or feet. Four people have to lay me on the floor and pull this gown on me. ON THE FLOOR. Then they stood me up. The designer says, 'Do you have a girdle?'

" 'NO, I DON'T HAVE A GIRDLE. NO.'

"Honest to God, I traveled to the Oscars on my back. I was in the back of the limousine lying down. How to get out? How? I asked the driver to please stop a block before and I *rolled* out. Isn't that unbelievable? I sat in the gown all night and I couldn't breathe. I was afraid the seams were gonna bust. If I leaned forward, I cut off my windpipe and I could just pass out.

"That's how I spent the night. Not to mention that there were six standing ovations, and every time we stood up, I had to be pulled out of the chair. PULLED OUT OF THE CHAIR. So I half lay in the chair all night, rigid. The one moment I didn't was when they read the nominees and the camera was on me. It was the worst."

"My best girlfriend was with me and she kept saying, 'How much is this gown costing you?' and I said, 'It has been drastically, drastically reduced. You can get this gown *real* cheap.'

"I have no pictures of it because I was the last person to enter the building. Because I was in a gown that was going to split. I was in a gown that had *to be cut off me*. Can you believe it?"

"I was so grateful to God that she [Angelica Huston] won, because that dress was so tight I would not have been able to walk up the seven steps to get it. As for my own loss, I didn't consider it a loss. I truly didn't consider it a loss. There was part of me that really wanted to win, and then there was another part of me, deep down inside that didn't, because to have won the very first time out would have been too much for even me—too much, too soon. I like growing in stages, and I like the idea of developing as an actress and I want to become a great actress. I might not have had that same kind of drive if I had won the Oscar the first time out; my perception of who I am might have changed. And as it is, I still have some places to grow and something to look forward to. I mean, I just haven't paid enough acting dues."

"I didn't win an Oscar. Perhaps God was saying to me, 'Oprah, you are not winning because your dress is too tight for you to make it up all those steps to receive the statuette.'"

Oprah had said three days earlier:
   "I'm not the least bit nervous about it actually. I don't get nervous about something when I have no control over it. Besides, my category is the first thing up, so I won't have to sweat it out all night."

On journalists asking to spend the day with her:
   "I turned them down for the same reasons I'm not wearing a purple gown. If you lose, you look totally ridiculous after they followed you around all day with a camera crew. And I'd look pretty stupid sitting there in that purple gown if I lost."

"I'm telling you, there aren't many black faces at the Oscars. So when you walk through the door, everybody looks around to see. 'Is it Lionel Richie? No. It's not Brenda Richie. Who is it? It's some black girl in a tight dress,' is what they say. And that's why I was so uncomfortable. I thought, 'Oh, God! Lionel Richie is gonna see me in this dress!' It was the tightest dress known to womankind. It was a horrible night."

Oprah Winfrey, Actress

Oprah told *Cosmopolitan*:

"Getting the Oscar nomination was pretty great. And I guess one of my biggest thrills was walking into the Oscar luncheon and sitting next to Jack Nicholson. He's my absolute favorite actor. I kept saying to myself, 'Self, would you look at this!'"

She did make it back to the Oscars, though, this time as a presenter. She told the audience:

"It's a lot easier on the nerves being a presenter than a nominee. You can concentrate on watching the show instead of spending three hours making your deals with God promising to go on a diet, to go to church, to stop biting your nails, and to stay out of shopping malls and everything in between."

Oscar night, 1995, she wore a Gianfranco Ferré gown and a diamond necklace and earrings:

"A lot of people offered to lend me jewelry for the night, but I didn't need it, honey—I got my own!"

"If you're ever going to dress, this is the night to do it."

DIET, WEIGHT, FITNESS

Food

"Food meant security and comfort. Food meant love. It didn't matter what you ate, just that you have enough. I've paid a heavy price for believing that."

"It's hell. Some days I want to buy a grocery store and eat everything in it!"

1989

"I used to brag, 'I don't ever get stressed.' I'd ask, 'What is stress? What does it feel like?' The reason I didn't get stressed is, I ate my way through it."

She recalled her fasting diet in 1988:

"I remember walking in the house once, and Stedman was playing Pac-Man, and I wanted him to pay attention to me. But he wasn't. I remember going to the refrigerator and standing there, staring and thinking, 'I got to eat. I got to eat. I got to eat.' That's when I first started to connect the thing about food and emotions."

"It's so hard—food is my drug and I just can't kick it. Part of me just wants to say, 'Forget it! Let me be me and let me do what I like to do: Eat!' But part of me hates me fat, hates me for piling on the pounds after promising I would be good!"

1990

"Now I'm trying to find a way to live in a world with food without being controlled by it, without being a compulsive eater. That's why I say I will never diet again."

1991

She spoke to Jane Pauley about the never-ending obsession of her life— food and weight:

"I was a total compulsive eater for most of my life. That's how I worked out my junk and other people work it out through alcohol or drugs or just bad relationships. So that's not my problem. You know, mine, you know, comes out in my hips. For me the weight is me try- ing to protect myself or feeling fearful or not being all that I really could be."

When asked by someone, *If you had one day in which you could be bad and there would be no consequences, what would you do?*:

"I would eat everything humanly possible without one single iota of guilt, without thinking about calories. I'd just enjoy it and take great plea- sure from all the grease on the potatoes."

Oprah did many shows on relationship problems. One topic was women's love affair with food:

"It is a very personal and a very painful subject for me because my weight . . . has been exploited by more tabloid articles than I care to count. For me weight is still an issue. I'd like to say it's not, but it is."

1992

"Isn't it the worst? I start out every morning with a poached egg and hope. By the end of the day the hope has faded . . . I luuuuuv food. You can tell by the span of my hips."

"I don't believe that most of us who are overweight are overweight because we've been eating healthily; it's because we eat what we like— barbecue ribs, french-fried potatoes, you know?"

"Obviously I have used food in the past to suppress my feelings rather than confront them. Even now it's hard not to. Having been a food addict, I can identify with the woman who is an alcoholic. I really, really understand people's pain."

From *In the Kitchen with Rosie* by Rosie Daley:
    "Changing the way you think about food is only the first step toward achieving and maintaining a desirable weight."

"My favorite meal is baked or broiled chicken breasts. I marinate them overnight in lemon juice and throw in every spice in the cabinet. Then I broil them with lemon juice and Worcestershire sauce. If you broil them until they're really, really crispy, they taste almost like they're fried."

"I had to retrain my taste buds. I come from a culture of people where you cook a green in pork fat covered in salt until it doesn't have no life anymore!"

1995

"I am a recovering foodaholic. It never goes away."

1996

Diets and Dieting

DIETS

"Three quarters of my life has been spent in a state of constant diet. I came to believe that if the food tasted good, it was loaded with calories. If something was good for you, and low in calories, it tasted that way. But now I realize that good-for-you food can taste good, too.

"What I've learned through my thirteen-year ordeal with weight is that you really can't begin to work on the physical until you first get at what's holding you back emotionally. The reason we don't move forward in our lives is because of the fears that hold us back, the things that keep us from being all that we were meant to be."

"I believe we were all brought to the planet for a purpose. It took me fifteen years to face my deepest fears, which I couldn't admit to anybody, including myself. My biggest fear was not being able to confront. I had a fear of not being liked. Plus I had a fear of saying no. I ruled my life by what other people wanted me to do. It was an emotional problem that manifested itself physically. I never really allowed myself to feel anything, because I covered it up with food."

"Eat reasonably, diet privately, and exercise regularly."

"My greatest failure was believing that the weight issue was just about weight. Dieting is not about weight. It's about everything else that's not going right in your life."

"I am one of those people who has dieted and gained, and dieted and gained, and since I started dieting, have gained seventy pounds. I wake up in the morning, I go and look in the mirror sometimes, and one of the reasons why I realized I don't have a handgun is because I would have shot off my thighs years ago."

"What we are all looking for, I think, is some kind of secret. And, you know, people say, 'Well, if they could put a man on the moon, they should be able to invent something.' I am still looking for the perfect answer. And that's why every diet book that comes out, I am still prey to that, too, because you read, and you think the answer's in this diet, or the answer's in that diet."

"I was much thinner before I started dieting. And now the goal weight that I wish for is what I was when I first started dieting. When I first started dieting, this is the truth. I first started dieting, this is about five or six years ago, and I was wearing a Calvin Klein size-ten jean. I thought that was bad, because I wanted to get into a size eight. I have those jeans, in memoriam, in my closet. They are there, and every year I say maybe I should give them away. But I won't give them away, because to give away Calvin Klein size-ten jeans means giving up a sense of hope, meaning that it's all over."

"I've done Diet Workshops, Weight Watchers, Diet Center [the 'banana, wienie, and egg diet'], the Beverly Hills Diet—I was a fool looking for papaya and kiwi—I've done all that. I gained six pounds on the Scarsdale Diet. I was out looking for lamb chops on Thursday and boiled eggs on Tuesday.

"From what I understand, it's part of my security system, because I've always said, 'Well, if this doesn't happen, it's because I was overweight.' It's a crutch. And I know it. I'm going to eliminate it as a problem in my life and then I'll have to find another problem."

DIETING

In 1988 Oprah went on a medically supervised liquid diet and lost sixty-seven pounds. She said that losing that weight

"was the single greatest achievement in my life."

When asked if she could maintain her discipline and stay slim, she responded:

"Asking me if I'll keep the weight off is like asking, 'Will you ever be in a relationship again where you allow yourself to be emotionally battered?' I've been there, and I don't intend to go back."

While on the Optifast Diet she cheated only once in Hawaii:
   "I became obsessed with having a cheeseburger."

"I've been dieting since 1977, and the reason I failed is that diets don't work. I tell people, if you are underweight, go on a diet and you'll gain everything you lost plus more. Now I'm trying to find a way to live in a world with food without being controlled by it, without being a compulsive eater. That's why I say I will never diet again."

1989

From her diary, 1989:
   "I've lost my resolve trying to find a way to carry on the battle."

"The absolute hardest part of dieting is doing it in the public eye.
   "Whenever I order something fattening to eat in a restaurant, they call the newspapers. It seems like they get the story before I have the meal delivered to my table!
   "One day I ordered apple pancakes in a restaurant and read about it in two newspapers the next day.
   "My biggest problem is that I love to eat—and no diet or exercise can take away the craving I have for fried foods and salty dishes.
   "This is the hardest thing I've ever done in my life. Anyone who says it's easy is lying. There is no easy way to keep off the excess pounds.
   "I hate exercising. It's torture for me. It's horrible, but what can I do? I have to continue. There are just too many people counting on me.
   "It's a fight that goes on every minute of the day. . . . I guess, for the rest of my life. But I'm not going back to my old fat self."

1989

"I'm tired of battling, battling, battling. I want a sensible diet to become part of my life forever."

"This diet's got to work—I've promised myself that."

"It was easy to lose weight with the liquid diet, but it takes so much energy to keep the weight off. People warned me this would happen, that liquid diets melt the pounds away, but they return when the dieting's over."

1990

"You know, there's an expression that goes 'There are only two things in life you can count on, death and taxes.' Well, believe me, you can add this one to your list: 'If you lose weight on a diet, sooner or later you'll gain it back.' "

1990

"I didn't do whatever the maintenance program was. I thought I was cured. And that's just not true. You have to find a way to live in the world with food."

1991

She stuck by her statement that she'd never diet again:
"I meant it because I now understand my eating and weight gains are symptoms of underlying emotional problems that dieting won't cure. Beneath my added poundage are buried feelings and my fear of feeling whatever they may be. That's the real issue and not the weight."

1992

"For so many years I wanted to look like Naomi Campbell, and before that I wanted to look like Diana Ross. There are days when I say it's not worth it to be a size ten. It's not worth it to run this hard, get up that early."

1995

"Dieting is not about weight. It's about everything else that's not going right in your life. It represents being out of control. And I like to control everything. But right now I'm learning to appreciate myself—my soul self and my spirit self—for what I have to offer and not trying to judge myself because of the weight. I'm trying to live in such a way that it's not an issue."

Why she had difficulty dieting:
   "It was because of my willingness to suppress my feelings. I could eat a feeling faster than anybody, put a little hot sauce on it and wouldn't recognize it until it showed up on my behind three days later."

1995

"The last year has shown me I really can do anything. All the years I used to talk about how you need to create a vision for yourself and you can achieve it, that is really true. It was difficult at first because I was betrayed a couple of times. But the betrayal taught me that you can survive anything. All the things you thought you couldn't handle, you can."

1995

"I knew it was time to do something when people asked me, 'How did you lose all the weight?' more than they asked, 'When are you and Stedman [Graham] getting married?' "

ROSIE DALEY

"Rosie changed my life."

In 1991 she hired chef Rosie Daley to act as a "diet cop" and help her lose weight:

"When I buy antiques, I get advice from experts, and when I need to hire directors or designers, I find out the best people, but with my weight I was struggling to do it myself. I realized I needed to get experts to help me. I like to eat, but I don't want my weight out of control. So I decided to hire a dietitian-cook—and found Rosie.

"I never want to return to my old eating habits. And by having someone twenty-four hours a day to monitor what I eat, and prepare only healthy foods for me, I think I'm at last on the right track."

"My cook, Rosie, was with me for two years before I lost one pound. It wasn't until last year that I was convinced that exercise works."

1994

"I've probably gained and lost hundreds of pounds. Now I know the only sensible thing is to eat less food and to work out and to get to the real heart of why you eat . . . you don't overeat because you're hungry."

1992

After presenting Rosie with the book's jacket photograph of the two of them together, Oprah grinned at her cook and declared:

"Merry Christmas—for life!"

Weight

⁓

"It is an obsession. It's all any overweight woman talks about. It just happens that I'm in the public eye, so people think I talk about it more."

1987

In July 1987 Oprah had shed almost twenty pounds and went on a shopping spree, buying clothes in new size fourteen:

"Now I've got to keep the weight off, or I'll have a closetful of expensive clothes that won't fit."

In October 1988 she was presented with the National Conference of Christians and Jews Humanitarian Award. She had lost a great deal of weight. Her father said that she told him:

"Dad, I took one look in the mirror and thought, 'Who's that—Diana Ross?' I get tears in my eyes when I think of my transformation. I hope I'm an inspiration to overweight women everywhere."

After her 1988 weight loss:

"I've let go of the fat which bound me. It was like having dust in my wings."

"People have said they liked me the other way, but they're lying, they're lying."

1988

"It's a comfort. I mean, some people go skiing and they go off to the Bahamas, and that's what they do for a vacation. I'm comforted by pasta.

"I get on a scale, and depending on whether it's up or down, it's going to be a good day or a not-so-good day, based upon the numbers, the numbers that control your life.

"It's painful. What people don't understand is it really is painful. So when people say to you, 'Why don't you just close your mouth? All it is is willpower. I lost five pounds in three days,' you want to slap them.

"You don't know what it's like unless food controls your life. For everything I put into my mouth, I either feel like 'Okay, I'm gonna let myself do this,' or I feel guilt about it. There's not one thing that I eat that I don't think about or regret later."

"I used to think that the reason I have this whole weight thing is because, I think, once I drop the weight—which I'm going to, so ya'll get ready and envy me, just envy me—one of the reasons I think I've held on to it is because, first of all, it gives people something to feel sorry for you about—because you have everything else, but you don't have great thighs, you see. So you use that so that they can't envy you because they have something you don't have."

"I said, 'I'm going to lose weight, I'm going to lose fifty pounds by Monday.' And so you know it's not going to happen, and so what does that do? That sends you off on another binge because you're not going to lose it the next day.

"I was wanting to lose all this weight so I could fit into the gown, and suddenly it dawned on me—what you need to do is lose thirty pounds in two days!

"So then I figured I might as well eat and enjoy the weekend."

"I feel like all of America is waiting for me to gain weight. It puts terrible pressure on me."

1989

"Taking my weight off was a picnic compared to the agony of maintaining this weight loss. I'm in the fight of my life!"

1989

"More than anything in my whole life I wanted to win the weight-loss battle. I want to show my audience and my friends that this is something anyone with the right motivation can accomplish."

1989

On November 15, 1989, one year after she reached her lowest weight, she devoted her show to a discussion of her constant struggle to keep from gaining back the weight:

"I promise after this show, I am never going to talk about this diet again. And if a reporter asks me about it, I'm going to start humming. I'm not saying another word about it."

In 1989 she wrote:

"I'm still battling what has been for me a lifetime struggle. I'm going to lick this, I just don't know how right now."

"I loved being slim—but I never got a chance to enjoy it because I started regaining so quickly.

"My body had learned to function on hardly any food, so as soon as I began to eat normally again, I packed on the pounds. I was angry and miserable. I started to hate my own body because I couldn't maintain that super shape that squeezed into size-ten jeans. I started to get depressed."

1990

By 1990 she claimed that she had come to terms with her weight:

"The weight is still a struggle for me, but I'm handling it. It is an illusion to think that going on a diet and dropping the weight can resolve whatever the weight problem is. Because it's more than just food. Holding on to the weight was for me a way of protecting myself. Covering myself. Weight has its purpose in my life. I haven't figured out what it is. When I do, I will have climbed another step. Won't that be wonderful! And I get a little closer every day to understanding it."

"Stedman says I've become a picky and irritable woman, the worst I've ever been, and he's probably right. He knows it's because I'm not happy with myself and my weight."

1990

"I'm carrying fat around. It's overcoming me. I woke up the past four days hating myself because I hadn't fasted or at least stuck to some kind of plan."

1990

"My greatest failure was in believing that the weight issue was just about weight. It's not. It's about not being able to say no. It's about not handling stress properly. It's about sexual abuse. It's all about the things that cause other people to become alcoholics and drug addicts."

1991

"I know I've been gaining a great deal of weight, but frankly I don't give a darn. I feel fine and fit and plan to live to be a hundred, regardless of my weight. But there's one area I'm sensitive about. I don't want to be a fat bride and have people snicker. So I've made it clear to Stedman that right now marriage is out. I'm not prepared to make the changes a man might want—like losing weight."

1991

By November 1993 she had finally gotten down to her target weight:

"Losing that weight was a metaphor for dropping extra baggage—physical, emotional, spiritual, and otherwise. Finishing a marathon would mean that I could do anything. It's been a dream of mine since I was thirty-two and in the heart of my weight struggles. In those days, as a fat person, I'd look at people running and wonder what it would take to do that. My dream was to do what once seemed impossible.

"But if I had known what it would take, I would have come up with another dream."

"Before now I didn't really deal with some of the deepest-rooted issues in my life. I thought I had. Because it was fairly easy to figure out my biggest problem, the reason I gained all that weight in the first place, and the reason I had such a sorry history of abusive relationships with men. I just needed approval so much. I needed everyone to like me, because I didn't like myself much. So I'd wind up getting involved with these cruel, self-absorbed guys who'd tell me how selfish I was, and I'd say, 'Oh, thank you, you're so right,' and be grateful to them. Because I had no sense that I deserved anything else. Which is also why I gained so much weight later on. It was a perfect way of cushioning myself against the world's disapproval.

"I remember after I first got to Chicago, I gained twenty pounds in the first two weeks. I thought I was handling the stress just fine. The show was going well. I was doing great. Everyone told me how easy I made it all look. But underneath I was terrified."

On the media prying into her weight-loss efforts:
"I know I brought that on myself. But come on, when is it enough?"

1993

While Oprah loves the attention from the public, she hates the attention to her weight:
"I'm just sick of it. We all make it an issue. I'm as guilty of that as anybody. I would like to reach a point where it is not an issue with me. I wish that I'd kept my weight off, but I do not feel like a failure. I feel like someone who has a weight problem. I feel like, oh, another forty million Americans who are dealing with this in their lives."

"This woman said to me, 'You better quit losing weight, because you're going to make the rest of us feel bad.' What she really meant was, 'Listen, if you start looking better than I do, I'm not going to like you anymore.' "

1994

"I used to walk into like a banquet or a convention or a seminar and I could feel it. I could sense people saying, "Oh she's got this and she's got that, but she's still fat, you know, and she has that good-lookin' boyfriend and she's doin' this and she's got all that money, but she's still fat.'

"And I understand it, I mean, I understand that it's absolutely human, a part of human nature, to want to see the negative in other people because it makes you feel better about yourself. I have to stop myself from doing it, you know. So I absolutely do understand how people can feel that."

People say that now that she's lost the weight, she's not the same:

"I don't believe that. And I remember there was a time when that would have really upset me, like the first time I lost weight, in 1988, on you know, that fast for four months, and people started to say that about me. I was really upset. I was unnerved by it. Now I'm a little older and certainly a little wiser.

"First of all, people don't even believe that themselves. They might think that, oh, because she's lost weight, I no longer relate to her. Because what it is about me that is relatable has nothing to do with weight."

In 1995 she regained ten pounds:

"Winter caught up with me. I wasn't willing to work as hard."

She vows to get back to what she calls "the ultimate Oprah":

"I do not believe I will go to a weight that's unhealthy for me again."

"For years I'd been saying on my show that you are so damned responsible for your life. You can't keep blaming somebody else for your dysfunction. Not your parents, not your mother, not your husband, not anybody. It really is about moving on. Then, as I entered my fortieth year, I realized that that belief applied to me, too. So I asked myself, if you want it so much, then why are you still fat.

"I was still afraid, even after all those years of talking about overcoming fears. I was afraid people wouldn't like me if I were thin, that the audience would turn on me. I was just so afraid to change. But I was also just tired of being stuck."

"I remember the last time I lost weight. Some woman said to me, 'Well, at least we still have Barbara Bush,' and I thought, 'Oh, no, they don't like me anymore.' I didn't deliberately go out and put the weight back on for that reason, but that concern was certainly embedded in my subconscious."

From *Ebony* magazine:

"My weight was always my apology to the world. It was my way of saying, 'Okay, I'm rich. I've got a good-looking boyfriend, and I've got a great life, but, see, I've got this big weight problem, so you can still love me.' "

"I don't feel like there's a fat person inside trying to get out. I feel like controlling my weight is about controlling my life, and if I allow my life to get out of control, my weight is a symbol of that. I am in my prime in the one-hundred-forty-eight to the one-hundred-fifty range. My thinking is clearer. My ability to focus and make decisions, my sharpness, my overall feeling about myself—everything is different."

1996

"It's a good thing for me to have actually put on an extra fifteen pounds because every time I think I got this weight thing licked, I recognize it's always there. My goal is to be in a Nike ad one day, running."

Health

"I decided a long time ago that I have to be healthy by the time I'm forty."

1993

"I thought I hated fruits and vegetables. Well, I've moved beyond apples.

"I'm happier than I've ever been and healthier. I'm losing the weight only for myself, not to please anyone else. I'm older now and I know, really know, that I don't have to have other people's approval to feel okay about myself. I can say no to people."

Fitness

After a forty-five-minute session on the Stairmaster plus sit-ups:

"Not too bad for a thirty-nine-year-old black chick, is it? Just a few pounds more."

1993

On working out:

"I'm doing it twice a day. Every day. Without fail. After my fast my metabolism slowed way down, so I have to rev it up every twelve hours.

That's what my trainer says. I figure any day now I'll be seeing some tabloid headline saying, 'Oprah's Overdoing It,' or 'Friends Fear Oprah's Getting Too Thin.' I'm going to frame those stories, I promise you that."

On her passion for exercise:
    "I'm like a diabetic who needs insulin."

On keeping up the pace of working out:
    "That is where I've changed. You have to make it a priority. Wherever you go, that's a priority."

                                                                        1994

Referring to personal trainer Bob Greene:
    "If Bob wants to push me, he'll say, 'See that woman in the pink suit? You can take her.' And I'll kill myself to run past her. I love to be under-estimated."

                                                                        1995

On running:
    "If I had more time, I'd only walk. It's certainly easier on your knees. The reason I run and do stairs is it's more intense."

"I am a weight-loss success because I am a life-change success. In the past I did everything but exercise to try to lose weight. I tried every program in the book, including a wienie, egg, and banana diet that made me sick after two weeks. I literally starved myself. And all I ended up doing was wrecking my physiology and metabolism. It wasn't until two years ago that I began exercising, and that's when I began losing weight and keeping it off."

                                                                        1995

"I have to work twice as hard as everybody else because my metabolism is so shot from years of dieting."

She told Jay Leno:
   "It's so hard, though. It's hard staying fit. I was huffing and puffing up the canyon today."

"At the end of the summer I was so tired, just run into the ground physically. I was Marcia Clark tired. I didn't know if I wanted to continue. I'm in the war all the time, and I was thinking, 'Well, I'm forty-one, and I've got every blessed thing in the world. Maybe I should just sit back and relax.' So when I was focusing on whether to stay [with the show], I was not as focused on my workouts."

1996

"It's a good thing for me to have actually put on an extra fifteen pounds, because every time I think I got this thing licked, I recognize that, like an alcoholic, it's always there. You've got to treat it like a dis-*ease*, an inability to deal with things as they come up."

RUNNING

In 1992 she completed a thirteen-mile race after losing sixty pounds:
   "People told me running would be fun. When I first started training, I said, 'What's fun about this?' But today was a lot of fun. That last mile was tough, but the goal was to finish. I may not have finished first in this

race, but I won nonetheless. I'm in the best shape of my life and I couldn't be happier."

"Running is the greatest metaphor for life, because you get out of it what you put into it."

"There's never a day when I say, 'I'm so glad to be out here at five A.M.' "
1995

"Who would have thought two years ago that I, Miss Two hundred and thirty-seven pounds, would be on the cover of *Runner's World*.

"Bob [her trainer, Bob Greene] figured out how to play on my competitive side. Once, during a short [6.2 mile] race I did in Charleston, South Carolina, last March, he overheard this guy in a pink shirt say he could not come home and tell his wife that he had let Oprah Winfrey beat him in a race. So Bob told me that, and I almost killed myself trying to beat the guy. I did, too."

THE MARATHON

In 1994 she completed the Marine Corps Marathon in Washington, D.C.:
"I never felt anything like the sense of accomplishment I had when I finished the marathon. But it's not really the race that mattered. It was the training, the discipline that it took to keep going for so many weeks beforehand. . . . I've been a 'whatever happens, happens' kind of person, just going with the flow. But running the marathon required goals and daily discipline, and follow-through. And I did it."

She ran her first (and, she says, last) marathon in Washington:
"Never did I feel I wasn't going to finish."

"I just tried to lose myself in it."

"I was the girl to beat. One guy had a T-shirt on that said, 'I Just Want to Beat Oprah.' "

As Oprah completed the twenty-six-mile run around Washington, she said,
"This is better than an Emmy."

"I think that's one of my great physical accomplishments. And that is not the actual running of the marathon in the rain in Washington, D.C., that day, but it is the twenty weeks prior to that, the discipline that it took to do that, is what I am most proud of. And it is the preparation. Just like in anything in life, it is how you prepare for it that allows you to be able to execute."

"You get to the twenty-second mile and you just try and lose yourself."

"Stedman, who once did a marathon, says he knows I can do anything I set my mind to. I actually inspired several people in my office to exercise."

She told Jay Leno:
"The tabloid guys ran with me."

"Actually it was the *National Enquirer*. They had two reporters train for the marathon. One ran the whole way, 26.2. And another came in at 13 miles. So they were right there really.

"It wasn't hurting. It was around the fourteenth mile I had to pee and I didn't know where the camera was.

"So, it was one of those—you know—personal little nightmares. Gotta go to the bathroom and there's the *Enquirer* right behind you.

"Well, it was one of the greatest accomplishments of my life. I started to cry at the end because it was the—I remembered all those years when I, you know, seeing images of myself in the mirror. And kind of waddling around and feeling the pain of the weight. Just the pain of, why can't I get control of my life? Why can't I do this? So I started to weep when I saw the twenty-six-mile marker."

"Training for the marathon was the hardest I've ever worked for anything. I'm not a person who usually sets goals; I usually move with the flow and act on instinct. But you can't do that with a marathon. You have to plan and work ahead of time. So this was one of my greatest challenges. It has been very, very difficult."

"Get Movin' With Oprah"

"Last Friday's program kicked off 'Get Movin' with Oprah: Spring Training 1995,' a six-week string of shows, each with a seven-minute nutrition and exercise break."

1995

"We decided to do this in May, recognizing that it was sweeps [month] and that [the] O. J. [Simpson trial] was going to be our number-one competition. If ever there was a chance to do something you felt was good for people without regards to what the numbers will be, this is it. Because I really don't know whether people will watch [this series] or not. But it's an O. J. month anyway, and you can't fight O. J., so what do we have to lose but a few thousand pounds across the country?"

"We want to get the whole country involved in spring training—getting moving. Getting America walking, that's my new thing."

On trainer Bob Greene:
   "He doesn't really have anything to sell, other than the concept of fitness. But I do think he'll get a few marriage proposals out of this."

"One of the things I'm trying to influence everybody in the country who struggled like myself is to understand that it is a life change. It's an ongoing process. It's not a diet that you wake up and start on Monday and by the end of the week you've lost ten pounds—it's a life change."

"I have gained such great respect for athletes. I never realized what discipline it takes. And I've developed greater respect for myself. That's one of the things I hope to share with people. How exercising makes you feel."

"This morning I felt redeemed. I was up late—I'm up watching *Nightline*, worried about the Oklahoma thing—I just can't let go of it— and I didn't sleep well, and I was thinking, 'God, I wish Bob [trainer Bob Greene] was one of those people I could call and say, "I can't do it today."' But I worked out, and I feel so much better!"

May 1, 1995

"I used to lie to myself. I had no honor. I was going to lose weight every January first. But you can't do that because you gotta have black-eyed peas on January first—all black people eat black-eyed peas on January first!"

"It's not a weight-loss program as much as a get-fit and get-moving program. I've been through every diet under the sun, and I can tell you that getting up, getting out, and walking is always the first goal."

"It meant there was an interest out there and that people wanted to get in shape, but that they didn't necessarily know the best way to achieve that goal. I empathized. As someone who has been on every diet known to man for the past eighteen years, I finally figured out that dieting alone wasn't the way to go about it."

"What I think about is, 'How am I going to get the energy to work out?'"

"My great hope is that this provides the breakthrough people need, that nudge to get started—or not. I mean, it's up to them."

LOVE AND MARRIAGE AND . . .

Love

⌒

"As a child, I was always trying to make myself loved. And the way I could receive what I thought was love was through achievement."

Asked about her love life:
   "I don't even have goldfish."

1986

"My father always said, 'When you fall, you fall so *hard*.' And it seemed to be true. I'd fall for some guy and it would be life or death. But maybe I've been in love once, truly in love."

1986

"I discovered I didn't feel worth a damn, and certainly not worthy of love unless I was accomplishing something. I suddenly realized I have never felt I could be loved just for being."

Men

During her time in Baltimore Oprah had a four-year affair with a married man:

"The more he rejected me, the more I wanted him. I felt depleted, powerless. Once I stayed in bed for three days, missing work; I just couldn't get up. Sad, isn't it?"

"There's nothing worse than rejection. It's worse than death. I would wish sometimes for the guy to die because at least then I could go to the grave and visit."

It was around this time, 1977, that Oprah began to develop a weight problem.

"I'd had a relationship with a man for four years. I wasn't living with him—I'd never lived with anyone—and I thought I was worthless without him. . . . At the end I was down on the floor on my knees groveling and pleading with him."

She described the breakup of a romance as:

"Worse than death. I have been down on the floor on my knees crying so hard, my eyes were swollen. Why? Why do we do this to ourselves?"

"Then it came to me. I realized there was no difference between me and an abused woman who has to go to a shelter—except that I could stay home. It was emotional abuse, which happens to women who stay in relationships that do not allow them to be all that they can be. You're not getting knocked around physically, but in terms of your ability to soar, your wings are clipped."

"I had so much going for me, but I still thought I was nothing without a man."

She identifies with audience members and their problems with men:
   "If you're a woman living, you've been done wrong by a man."

In her twenties she was "powerless and pitiful," waiting for that guy to call:
   "Wouldn't even bathe because I thought if I ran the bathwater, I wouldn't hear the phone ring."

"Now I'm free! And the man who caused me so much pain now says, 'I want to marry you.' [She laughs.] And I say, 'Who doesn't?'"

On her love life:
   "There's nobody right now, but he's coming—I know it. My idea of heaven is a great big baked potato and someone to share it with."

1985

"You don't have a man, you need spaghetti."

1986

"The 'Oprah Winfrey' factor always came in. If it didn't go away, he went away."

"People think because I'm in television, I have this great social life. Let me tell you. I can count on my fingers the number of dates I've had in the four years I've been in Baltimore, and that includes the ones I paid for."

"I think that I'd be really great with some guy; but, you know, I'm not going to go around hoping and praying for it anymore. If it happens, it happens. If it doesn't, I'll get a kitten."

1986

"It's really difficult being a career woman and finding someone who is equally as smart and doesn't mind you being smart. I used to worry about it all the time. I really don't anymore. I believe it will come when it's time."

On her search for affection, she mentions a recent tip from one of her guests:

"The best place to find single men these days is the frozen-food section of the supermarket around seven P.M. So, everybody, see ya there!"

She told *People* magazine:

Someone tells you you're wonderful, you wonder what's wrong with them. Somebody tells me I'm horrible, I'd say, 'This is wonderful. He understands me. I can grow.' I'd have some arrogant egomaniac dog telling me I was too self-centered, and I'd be thinking, 'Thank you so much for telling me. I need to work on that.' "

"But my staff kids me 'cause they say, you know, the reason I can interview all these people is because I think I'm every woman, and I've had every, you know, malady, you know, and I've been on every diet and I've had, oh, men who have done me wrong, honey. So I—I relate to all of that, and I'm not afraid or ashamed to say it. So whatever is happening, if I can relate to it personally, I always do."

1987

"I have been in the backseat with some Negro with his hand on my breast—talking about, 'Baby, you don't have to,' in one breath and the next minute saying, 'If you love me, you really would.' But had I not said no, I could be in a position that would never have allowed me to be able to do the things, be all that I can be right now, because when I was seventeen, Lord, if William Taylor had married me, I'd have been married to a mortician right now, because that's what he is. I'd have been married to a mortician and probably teaching Sunday school in—in Nashville someplace, because I wanted him. I wanted him. Lord, I wanted him, threw his keys down the toilet. I wanted him, stood in front of the door and threatened to jump off the balcony if he didn't stay. I wanted him. I was on my knees begging him, 'Please don't go, please don't go.' To this day I thank God he left."

"From now on I'm living this life for Oprah, not for some man. Women diet to keep their men, everybody knows that. But I've decided men can go to blazes. Why should I spend the rest of my existence worrying about some silly man ? If he doesn't want me the way I am, he can take a hike. The charade is over. I'm going to be the Oprah I always wanted to be: fat and sassy!"

1990

"I don't want anything to do with men now, and that includes starting a family with one. To hell with guys. I'd rather be fat and happy than miserable with someone who can't accept the real me."

"I no longer feel . . . that I have to have a man in order to make myself whole—I feel there are important discoveries yet to be made."

"I'll tell you what frustrates me the most. What frustrates me the most is these women who still live their lives for men. I want to just shake them sometimes! But I've been one of those women, so I understand. I understand that you have to come to it in your own time, and that it just takes some of us longer than others. And so you may have six children and three husbands before you can figure it out."

"I often say in speeches that we have a whole country of women, people who are trying to live a Hanes panty-hose existence, because we've heard that gentlemen prefer Hanes."

From *Entertainment Weekly*, September 9, 1994, when asked, *Do you ever look back to someone who wronged you and think, 'Hey, sucker, look at me.' Or are you beyond that?*

"I'm not beyond that. Are you kidding? I was just reading my old journals last night, and there was this one entry I couldn't remember writing. Lots of others I can remember, you can see the tears on the pages. But there was this one where I was writing about not being able to do enough for this guy. I think I was twenty-four at the time, and I was writing, 'Maybe if I was rich enough or famous enough or was witty, clever, wise enough, I could be enough for you.' And now I'm thinking, 'I hope he is sick every time he sees me on TV.' This is a guy I used to take the seeds out of the watermelon for so he wouldn't have to spit!"

MR. RIGHT

She spoke to Mike Wallace on *60 Minutes* in 1986—on meeting Mr. Right:
"It will happen, I keep saying, but now I say to myself, if I lose forty pounds, maybe it'll happen then. Then maybe it'll happen. You know, I have ... before the movie, I said, 'After the movie it'll happen.' Then, 'Before the Oscars it'll happen.' I don't know. I think it will. If it doesn't, I might come a-calling on you."

"Mr. Right's coming, but he's in Africa and he's walkin'."
                                                              1986

Oprah once told her audience:
"This is what we've heard, 'You just really need to stop looking and putting pressure on it' I've been told that. 'The minute you stop looking, you will find him.' I've gone to many a banquet I didn't want to go to because I thought, 'Maybe he'll be here.' You walk into a room and you say, 'Okay, God, I'm not looking, but ...' "

"If there is a six-foot-two-inch black man who fits this category, please, please *come* in!"
"No, I haven't given up yet. But I've stopped worrying about it. I think that if you're an intelligent, successful black woman in the eighties, you're going to have a difficult time finding a mate who is supportive. Mr. Right

either will or will not happen for me, and I'm not going to stand still waiting for him.

"[Mr. Right would be] taller than me, smarter than me, and not threatened by me. He would have to be outgoing but know when to shut up. And I don't think it would matter if he was black, white, or Chinese."

"It's very important for me to have a man I can look up to. I like them tall and I like them smart. [That combination] is not an easy thing to find, but it will happen."

"I don't need the kind of 'dating' when you're going out with a man just to go out. If it's not going to be a meaningful relationship—and I can tell you in three minutes if it is or not—then I don't waste my time. So I go through periods where I don't see anyone. Like now. It's not intentional, just sort of a de facto celibacy.

"Actually I believe you can have it all, but I also believe that nothing happens before its time. And maybe I'm just not ready to have a man in my life right now. But it's the saddest thing. I'll tell you, that's been the price. That has definitely been the price."

Stedman Graham, Jr.

Recalling the beginning of her romance with Stedman Graham, 1985:

"I asked the Spirit, 'Lord, could you do something about this man situation in my life? I get so tired of runnin' into these no-good men who don't have a job and want my money.' So I asked the Spirit, 'Would you send me somebody? Lord, could he be smart? Could he have some intelligence? And if you don't mind, could he be tall?' And the Spirit, he sent me Stedman."

"At first I wasn't really that interested because, for one, I still had doubts about myself. He's a very attractive man. And I was thinking that kind of man usually goes for cupcakes—one of those women with long hair who has had her nose done. Actually he called three times over a period of time. The first time I stood him up. The second time I made excuses. Finally, the third time, he said, 'I'm not going to ask you anymore.' So I went out with him.'

When Stedman first asked her out, her staff warned her against dating him:

"They figured if he looked like that, he had to be either a jerk or want something."

The morning after her first date with Stedman, she exclaimed to her coworkers: "I'm so glad I went! He bought me roses, paid for dinner, and was interested in what I had to say!"

About turning down Stedman when he first asked her out:

"He's so handsome—oooh, what a body—so I figured, if he's calling me, either he's a jerk or there's something wrong with him I should know about."

"He's kind and he's supportive, and he's six feet six inches!"

Love and Marriage and . . .

She told Barbara Walters on *Good Morning America*: "I think it's pretty serious. It's great fun. He's very kind and supportive."

Reminded by Barbara Walters that she had once told her she didn't think she'd meet Mr. Right, Oprah answered:

"You're right. Up until seven or eight months ago I said it would never happen. I have my career. I'll go on and live my life and that'll be fine.

"I think what happened is what I read about in all the women's magazines. They say if you stop looking, you can find it."

"One thing that makes our relationship great is we laugh a lot."

1987

In an interview for *Essence* magazine in August 1987, she described her relationship with Stedman:

"The greatest thing about him is his kindness. And he knows who he is. I am thrilled that I have discovered this in a black man."

"He's as kind as he is tall. He's my number-one fan, and he isn't jealous of my success. In a relationship where one person is always in the public eye, it can be hard for the other person—particularly if it's the man—to be able to stand back and say, 'Okay, you go for it if you want to.' But he can, and that means a lot to me."

1987

"Face it, when a man like Stedman—as good-looking as Stedman—starts dating a woman like me, people are going to talk.

1987

"Many times we are prejudiced for or against people based on their appearances. And I just assumed that because he was six-six and has a beautiful physique and could have just about any woman he wanted, and I have these physique problems, why would he choose me? And I assumed that he'd be arrogant and obnoxious and self-centered and so forth. But he's just the opposite. He's one of the kindest . . . one of the reasons we're still together is because of his patience and his kindness. And he is honorable. Like my father, just honorable."

An ugly rumor arose about Stedman, which stemmed from false rumors that he was gay:

"It is a vicious, malicious lie, and no part of it, absolutely no part of it, is true. . . . I have chosen to speak up because this rumor has become widespread and so vulgar that I just wanted to go on record and let you know that it is not true."

She blamed herself for the rumors:

"I believe in my heart that had I not been an overweight woman, that rumor would never have occurred. If I were lean and pretty, nobody would ever say that. What people were really saying is why would a straight, good-looking guy be with her?"

"He was so brave, and I have never loved him more."

"He's the best man who's ever been in my life. I have that love glow when I'm around him. You know the old cliché, 'A good man is hard to find'? Well, it's true. And the smarter you get, the harder they are to find. Stedman is right for me."

1989

In 1989 Oprah introduced Stedman to her audience:

"So much that's been written about this relationship is untrue, and I thought it was time to clear the air. I want people to meet Stedman for themselves and get a feel for what our relationship is all about. I also want people to get a sense of what it's like for him, or any private person, to maintain a relationship with a person who's constantly in the public eye."

By late 1989 Oprah was deeply involved with Stedman. She even took up golf:

"I really hate golf, but I'll chase those little white balls around because it's what he likes."

There were problems with a long-distance romance:

"With Stedman based in North Carolina and me in Chicago, we only have weekends together. All that's going to change next year when Stedman moves to Chicago."

"We've just never hashed out where our lives were going. Then one morning while I was running I realized our relationship had no direction and that I wanted more.

"I couldn't stand it any longer. I called Stedman and told him we needed to sort this thing out right away. I said, 'Steddy, I want to come to North Carolina and nail you down for life.'"

"It gets better the more time we spend together. We get excited going to the grocery store.

"Stedman is ideal for me. I can't imagine or think of—nor have I ever seen or experienced—anybody who would be more ideal for me."

1990

"He knows that sometimes I'm home, but I'm not really there. My mind is in a hundred other places. And he doesn't want that for a wife, and I don't want that for him. He wants somebody who's going to make him the most important, and that's what he should have. There'll come a time when this settles a bit. The paint isn't even dry on the [studio] front hallway yet."

In 1990 Oprah told a family insider:

"I'd always been opposed to living with a man, but I realized how much I wanted to be with Stedman.

"I didn't want to just squeeze him in now and then any more than he wanted to hang around like a poor puppy dog, waiting for a moment alone with me."

"It's tough to have a relationship with someone like me. And the older I get, the tougher I am. . . . Because I control so many things in my life, I have to work at not being controlling when I'm spending time with Stedman.

"I don't understand why Stedman can love me so at this weight because I think, 'You could have any thin girl you wanted.' "

1992

"He is the first man I have ever known who truly wants me to be not only the best I can, but all I can be. He knows in the past I caved in to pressure because I felt I hadn't the right to say no. Because I always felt just being Oprah wasn't enough. I had the need to always please others, to win their approval, and to be admired. Often at my expense. No more. With Stedman's help I've learned to be true to myself.

"Stedman knows that I'm not impressed by money, although surely I once was. Now that I have all the things I once thought would make me happy, they have little meaning for me. Experience, and not just a little heartache, has taught me money buys convenience and conveniences. I'm not knocking it, either, but life's true meaning is about the time you spend comfortably with your mate—and with yourself."

1992

In 1992 on winning her third Emmy:
"Thank you, Stedman, for putting up with all the long hours."

In 1993 Oprah did two shows about her weight, chronicling how she had bicycled, run, and hiked with the help of personal trainer Bob Greene and ate tasty but low-fat meals prepared by chef Rosie Daley. At the end of her story Stedman came onstage:
"I just wanted America to know that Stedman has loved me no matter what size I was. [She looked at him directly.] You stood by me and loved me no matter what—and I thank you for it."

She confesses to being slow to express gratitude for having Stedman in her life:
"I feel bad about this. I haven't been as nurturing and affectionate with him as I would have been had he treated me worse.

"Throughout my life I have done the most incredible things for men who treated me like s——. For my first boyfriend I remember going into the kitchen and making an omelet. If it was a little lopsided, I threw it out and started over, to make sure it was perfect. But now I'm attracted to somebody who doesn't require that. Where I don't have to say, 'Look, look, I'm good—will you stay, please?' I really do think I don't do enough for him."

Asked, *Then why does he stick around?*
"I'm a neat girl."

1993

"We're very happy. This impression that we've broken up and gotten back together and broken up again, it is absolutely, categorically not true. Not true! Not true! It's a media-created story. Let me say again, it is not true. We have never broken up. Not once."

1993

Oprah understood people's reaction to her relationship with Stedman:
"People ask questions and they are going to come up with their own answers. [such as] Money. They look at him and they look at me and they think, *'Money. That's what he sees in her'*—but they're wrong. They're way off! Way off! Stedman is the most independent, the most stubborn, the most proud. . . . That man wouldn't take a nickel from me. Not that he needs to."

"Stedman's my rock. He's an honorable man, fair, moral, decent, and kind. He'll go out of his way to do anything for you."

1994

Love and Marriage and . . .

From a *Good Housekeeping*, October 1995, interview with Liz Smith, when asked, *You have managed to have a long relationship with a handsome, intelligent man who isn't after your money:*

"That's the best thing. He is his own man. He's really not interested in the boyfriend-fiancé title. He's interested in creating his own life separate from mine. But he says if I want to run for president, he would work on the campaign. I don't think you can have it better than that!"

Calling Stedman "an overwhelmingly decent man," Oprah told *Ebony*:

"He has made me realize a lot of the things that were missing in my life, like the sharing that goes on between two people."

"Stedman is very ambitious and driven. He's very different from me in that he's very vision-oriented and sets goals. I live in the moment and expect it to carry me. And one of the things I admire and love about him is that once he gets something or figures it out, he always wants to give back and share. And he feels very strongly about the sports world and particularly athletes being able to work beyond athletics."

"I don't think I'd be with him, though, if he didn't hate the limelight so much. Frankly most of the men I've dated would have loved to be in that limelight. People said when we first started going out that he was after my money or trying to get an acting job, and it was so disheartening because just the opposite was true."

1995

About his book, *Ultimate Guide to Sport Event Management and Marketing*, Winfrey said:

"I haven't read it cover to cover yet. But I've read his parts. And I thought it was wonderful."

"I do believe that if I had been quote thin from the beginning, there wouldn't have been the suspicion about 'Why is such an attractive, intelligent man with this woman?' "

"He'll be a wonderful father. He really gives me a glow. Sometimes I look at Stedman and I just can't stand it. I go, 'Oh, my heart, be still.' "

"He not only washes the dishes, he cooks. Best of all, he's not famous. Lots of people want to ride with you in the limo. But you want someone who'll be there when the limo breaks down, who'll help you catch the bus."

1985

"He just plain sees me, not the size."

"He's out of town more than I am. It used to be the other way around.
    "The relationship is better than it has ever been, because he feels confident and strong about the work he is doing."

"Last night Stedman and I were sitting on the sofa and I was saying, 'Gee, you have a lot more fun than me.' He was about to go to Telluride [Colorado] for the weekend with his golf buddies. I was about to face a weekend of long runs."

"But he's in different cities all the time. I tell him, 'I'll meet you at the American Airlines counter.' "

"I hated myself because of my weight, but I want America to know that my fiancé, Stedman Graham, has loved my heart and loved me no matter what size I was. He stood by me."

"Yes, I am definitely in love, and it's a wonderful feeling. The success of my show is great, losing weight is great, but nothing compares with being in love. Zippity-doo-dah, I'm in love!"

Appearing as a guest on Gayle Bumpus's show on Hartford station WFSB:
    "Well, Gayle was there the weekend that Stedman proposed."

"Stedman's the best thing that has happened to me. I want to spend the rest of my life with him. But I love him too much to marry him."

"Stedman is always in control. When he has a goal, he meets it. I have to say that he is the one person I know who did not see the Bronco chase. He called me from a library in [Washington] D.C. the night O. J. [Simpson] was in the Bronco. And I go, 'Are you watching?' He's like, 'Watching what? I'm in the library.' I said, 'You've got to get to a TV.' He said, 'I'm not going to a TV. I'm doing research.' And I'm screaming, 'Get to a TV.' But he never saw it. He never left the library. That's how calm he is. When he's got his mind set on something, he just does it."

1995

"It's gotten to the point where Stedman and I now have itineraries. His secretary faxes my secretary where he's going to be, where I'm going to be, so that at some point we can be together. It's gotten that bad."

1996

Love and Marriage and ...

THE "MARRIAGE QUESTION"

Before she met Stedman, she told interviewers that she had written in her daily journal in 1986:

"I'm not married. I'm *never* going to be. . . . Lord, could you do something about this man situation in my life?"

"It was not a happy day when I found out about the Yale University study saying that women not married by the age of forty have a greater chance of being killed by a terrorist than walking down the aisle to say, 'I do.' I tell you, I wore a black armband for a week mourning that one," Oprah commented as her audience laughed in appreciation.

While Oprah said she didn't feel any pressure to get married, she also said:

"My friends tell me, 'Three years into a relationship, you have to decide.' And I'm getting that old biological clock pressure, too."

"We're not married because I'm not ready to be married. Real marriage is the sacrificing of your ego, not for the other person, but for the relationship. That's how you become one, because the relationship becomes the number-one priority. I am really not in that place."

1990

"Because I'm not ready to be married. That's the real reason. Everybody's desire for me to have a wedding has nothing to do with my knowing I'm ready to be a wife. That's a whole different responsibility that I can't handle right now.

"Now, I feel like he has his life, I have my life. It's fine just like it is. It's a different kind of commitment. You know, Joseph Campbell said that marriage is really the sacrificing of the ego for the relationship. When I'm ready to put myself in that position, I will. I've done so many shows about marriage and divorce and relationships that have failed. I know it would be foolish to think you can have it all in one time. I think you can have it all. You just can't have it all at once."

1990

"I'd say we are closer to it now than we've ever been. And that's the best answer I can give."

1992

"I'm allowed great personal freedom in the relationship right now, and I think that if I'm married, as good as Stedman is, I think that his expectation of what I should be would change. I really do. 'Cause I think he's pretty old-fashioned in that respect. You know, that a 'wife' ought to be home sometimes, and I'm not ready for that right now."

1992

"The only reason we would marry is to have children. I do want children. But not now. There are still too many things to do—and I enjoy the courtship."

1992

"Frankly a piece of paper legalizing what Stedman and I have together couldn't make it any better than it already is. So, unless we decided to have children, it wouldn't bother me if we never got married."

1992

"Everybody's, like, in my business. They're, like, 'Well, when are you going to get married?' and 'Why aren't you married?' and 'So what are you waiting on?'

"If Stedman looked differently—he's really quite a handsome guy. And I think if he looked differently, if he were, you know, squatty, or, you know, if he were as overweight as I am, people wouldn't say that [that he's going to break Oprah's heart]. It's really—it's really, really, very sexist."

In 1992 she spoke to her friend Gayle about the "marriage question":

"It does scare me a little bit, the whole idea of being married to somebody for the rest of your life. You don't want to wake up ten years from now and say, 'My God, who is this I've married?' So it scares me a little bit, but I think it's the right thing to do."

"Okay, let's get it over with: We are still getting married. But we did not set a date. Never. Let me say it again: We did not set a date. So how can we have put it off? That was a notion concocted out of thin air by the press. It has nothing to do with the truth of Stedman and me."

1993

Referring to a prenuptial agreement, which Stedman insisted on:

"Which we haven't signed yet."

1993

Does she have continuing qualms about marriage?

"No. But you know, obviously I've seen a lot of disrupted relationships on my show. So I asked Stedman the other day, 'Tell me, what does marriage mean to you?' And he said, 'It means everything will be exactly the same as it is now, but better.' And I said, 'Whoa, there, what do you mean "better"?' And that made me think. It made me say to myself, 'Maybe we both need to be absolutely clear about what this whole marriage thing means.' So I said to Stedman after that, 'Well, then, what do you think a wife is?' And he said, 'She is the person who is there for the man that she loves.' And, you know, I thought that was just beautiful—I said to him, 'Baby, you are so great'—because that's what I think a good husband is, too: the person who is there for the woman he loves. Isn't that beautiful?

"But that's hard for me at the same time, hearing him say that. Because literally I can't always be there for him. I work a lot. I will never be the good, traditional wife, at home a-cookin' and a-cleanin.' And he knows that. But it does make things hard. It's lucky we have a real commitment between us. I love him. He loves me. When you have that, marriage doesn't seem as important. It's more a matter of 'We'll get to it when we have a minute.' There, is that enough?"

In a February 1994 interview:

"There was a time in my life when I needed marriage to validate myself, but now I'm very content with what my relationship gives me. I'm very sorry I ever mentioned Stedman's name to the press. This whole wedding thing might not be such a big issue if I had never mentioned it. But if I hadn't, then everybody would be asking, 'Who's the mystery man?' 'Is she a lesbian?' "

"Neither of us is ready. It really bothers me that people think it's either he doesn't want me or I don't want him."

1995

"Marriage is no longer the number-one question, though. It's been replaced by my weight loss. I think before, because I was overweight, people wondered how I could go out with someone so good-looking. They sought ulterior motives."

1995

On the "marriage question":
   "It hasn't come up, and we're doing just fine."

1995

She sees marriage
   "as a commitment to work on yourself with somebody and say, 'Look, you're going to be there for me no matter what, and I'm going to be there for you, no matter what.' I'm saying it now in the relationship. I don't see marriage as the illusion of living happily ever after."

"I thought I was over that marriage question. I don't know when I'm getting married. I really don't know. I don't know if I'm getting married. I really, really don't know."

"If you've all noticed or watched over the years, I don't wear rings. I've only ever wanted one ring [a wedding ring]."

[211]

She says she should have kept her "big fat mouth" shut about marrying Stedman:

"Slap myself on my nonring finger. We'll get married when both of us are ready. And neither of us seems to be ready."

"The truth is I'm in no hurry. In spite of all the worldly pressure for me to have a wedding, I no longer feel what I felt many years ago—that I had to have a man in order to make myself whole."

1993

ON HAVING CHILDREN

Asked if she would have a child without marriage:

"No. And I don't have any particularly strong moral aversion to people who do. I think that's fine. If that's what you want. But I want the kind of life I didn't have. I want the father. I want June and Ward Cleaver. I want a father who comes home and is happy to be there. And I want to be there loving and nurturing my daughter or my son. I want my daughter or son to grow up with a father in the home who knows that he or she is loved. That's what I want. . . . And I want the kind of bonding and commitment that marriage brings. I want real intimacy. I want my husband to be a friend as well as a lover. And so I want my children to know that I love their father and he loves me. I don't want to be afraid to talk about sex, have sex, and all of that. So. No. I wouldn't have a child without being married."

1988

"It has to do with sharing all I know now with someone from the time that person was born. It has to do with contribution and extension and growth. I relish the thought of trying to raise a child. I'm curious to see what it would be like to raise a child, teaching him responsibility, a sense of caring, but also independence."

1989

"I want to raise a child who understands he or she is created from goodness and power in the light of God and can do anything he sets his mind to."

1989

"Some days I really want a girl because you can dress her up and she'd be so cute—she'd be like me. Then I think I'd want to have a boy because I'd like to name him Canaan. Canaan Graham is such a strong name."

1989

In 1990, on the possibility of children:

"I certainly have no business having children at this time. Time is running out, I know, but I'm going to give myself a few years. Got too many other things going."

"Sometimes I think, yes, I do want to have that experience. And other times I must admit having a child is not a deep yearning at this time. Maybe I'm afraid. Raising a child is such a serious business."

1991

"You have to be emotionally mature and responsible. And I'm not sure I'm describing me when I say that, at least not yet. But I'm getting there."

1992

In 1992, on the question of children and the biological clock:

"It's getting loud, but there are so many little black children out there. . . . If I reach the point where the clock has gone dead on me, I will just adopt children."

"The truth? I love children. But right now, with my life the way it is, I just can't see myself having any. Having children is synonymous with sacrifice, I think. Don't get me wrong. It's a noble sacrifice. I am in awe of good mothers. But I don't feel I can do that right now. You have to be there for the children all the time. I can't even do that for my dogs. So I've decided for now to stick with that aunt or friend-of-the-family thing, where you get to have a blast with the kiddies for a while, then say to Mom, 'Here you go; they're all yours.' "

1993

"I would never have children without the benefit of marriage—the benefit for them—as I recall all too well what it is like to be an illegitimate child. Also, with a child but without a marriage, how could I speak before the thousands of teenagers I address each year and advise them not to bear children unless they are married? It does not matter that I can well afford to take care of a hundred as easily as one child without a husband. I would still feel the hypocrite."

1994

Asked about her biological clock:

"So, yes, it's ticking. So what? It's what I'm doing in this moment that really matters, and if I am supposed to have children, I will, and I will know that."

"You know I'm forty-one," she says, noting that her biological clock, which she once described as "a gong" has "gone beyond the sound barrier now. But I don't feel it's the time for me [to have children], so I feel that time is literally going to run out."

1995

"Sometimes when I'm running, I'll think, 'Why don't I feel that pressure?' Because I know there are so many little black children out there that if you just want a child, you will always be able to have a child. And I am not hung up on 'What if I don't have the baby myself?' "

"Having a child come from my body isn't as important to me as being able to change the life of a child. There are so many little black children out there I would adopt in a second."

"I do not believe that I have at this time in my life what it takes, the natural ability to handle a child. Some people have that. They just were born—all their lives they wanted to have children. Or the commitment to sacrifice that it also takes. I do not have it. So therefore I should not be . . . a person bringing a child into the world. And all the people who say, 'Oh, but you could, and you could bring the baby to work and roll it around the studio.' That is not what I should do. I should use myself, my voice, my life, to try to uplift and change the lives of as many other children as I can."

"I would be afraid that I don't have the courage, at this time in my life, to follow through, to do it the way it needs to be done. I do believe that it is the most, I mean the honorable job that there is and also that mothers are really the true spiritual teachers."

"I have such respect for people who stay home and care for their children. That is the most important job in the world, and the problem is that we just pay lip service to that.

"What it takes to be a good mother is not what this life that I lead right now is.

"All these people who say you can bring the baby to work and you can have the baby in your life, well, that's sacrificing to the child."

"I would say I'm not going to have kids. What it takes to do it right, I don't have it. I think it would be immensely unfair to bring a child into the world and expect that child to fit into my lifestyle."

"I don't think I'd be a very good mother. I think motherhood is the most important thing there is, and those who take on the role better be ready to make it a full-time job, and I'm just not up to that."

To Jay Leno on *The Tonight Show*, February 1995:
    "Having a puppy has really kind of cured me of the whole desire."

Love and Marriage and . . .

Puppy Love

Oprah's love extends to animals, especially dogs ("I love dogs!"). At her Indiana farm she has Labrador retrievers and golden retrievers (she once showed off a whole basketful of puppies to her TV audience), and a dog who followed her home ("and is he glad he did!").

For Christmas 1994 Stedman gave her a cocker spaniel puppy named Solomon. She told Larry King on *Larry King Live*, January 4, 1995:

"It is the best present I ever got. Now, I have a lot of—I have dogs at the farm. I have great big old golden retrievers, and we have some black labs there, but this is my city dog, Solomon. I've been up in the middle of the night walking him. We're almost potty trained."

She spoke to Jay Leno on *The Tonight Show*:

"It works the way it is and it's fine. He [Stedman] gave me the best present of my life, you know. The dog. [She then brings her new puppy, Solomon, onstage.] You can't bring a new baby to work every day, but I can bring Solomon."

From America Online, October 3, 1995, when asked, *Are you really going to adopt a baby, or is that just a mass media rumor?*

"I just adopted another dog. Mass-media rumor big-time! Maybe they got it confused. I have a new black spaniel named Sophie. She's Solomon's pal."

OPRAH HERSELF

Self-Image

"There were certainly times as a child when I felt, 'My God, I wish I were like everybody else.' But as an adult I celebrate my upbringing. I say, 'Thank goodness I was raised by my grandmother the first six years, then sent to live with my mother and then with my father. Because of the various environments I was exposed to, I am better able to understand what others have gone through."

There was an article about her in *Newsweek*'s December 31, 1984, issue. Oprah found herself uncomfortable, however, when the magazine described her as "nearly two hundred pounds of Mississippi-bred black womanhood, brassy, earthy, street-smart and soulful":

"I did not like it. I don't like the term *street-smart*. I think it's a term that gets put off on black people a lot. Rather than say intelligent, it's easier to say we're street-smart and that kind of explains a lot of things. 'Oh, well, she made it because she's street smart.' Well, I am the least of the street-smarts. I've never lived on the streets. I don't know anything about it. I never was a hustling kid. I mean, I had my days of delinquency. But I was never like a hustling kid or streetwise. I wouldn't last ten minutes on the streets."

"I'm slow to anger. I'm not an angry person. I have always been the kind of person who believed no matter what happens to me, I have to be responsible for changing it. I never blame other people for anything that happens to me."

"I am not blond and I am not thin."

"I have a gift. I understand that it's a gift, to be myself in front of the camera. I am as comfortable in front of the camera as I am breathing. You know, the little red light comes on. It's like, 'Hey there, how are you doing?' The first day I did it, I came off the air and I said, 'This is it.' "

"My ability to acquire things has changed, but *I* don't feel any different. So I keep saying to myself, 'Well, I guess I'm not a star yet, because I don't feel like one.' "

1987

"Right now I feel about as good as you can feel and still live."

1987

"I wanted to be somebody. And I think perhaps maybe I've been so busy just being that person that this is one of the first times I've thought, yes, yes, I have done that. I have done that. To have gotten there and know that you worked to get there. And that wasn't easy. It really wasn't easy. It feels very good."

1988

"I really do get hurt when I hear people doing 'fat' jokes."

"I probably would not, without my past, sexual abuse included, be able to handle what's happening to me as well as I think that I am."

"I was walking down the street yesterday and I see this little round butterball of a lady. She leans over the balcony and hollers at me, 'Let's hear it for fat women!' I guess I haven't come as far as I thought.

"I got my weight from my grandfather cows, my aunt cows, and my cousin cows.

"I do have black-women's behind. It's a disease God inflicted upon the black women of America."

"I'm lucky because I live in the public eye and people treat me positively. But there are also people who think they can one-up me. They say, 'She may have a talk show, she may have been nominated for an Oscar, but she's still got fat thighs!' "

"I carry it well. But it's driving me nuts. I'm five-six. In Baltimore, I weighed one-forty-eight. When I was Miss Tennessee, I weighed one-thirty-five. You can see my bones at one-thirty-five. But when I moved to Chicago, I started *really* putting on the pounds. I think I wanted that weight as a defense, so if the show failed, I could blame it on that. Same thing with me. As long as I'm heavy, I've got a great excuse. But I tell you, this is the biggest, biggest problem in my life. Not being able to have the self-discipline to beat this. It truly makes me really *depressed*."

In a commencement speech at Morehouse College, 1989:

"I, like a lot of people here, spent a lot of time trying to be somebody I was not. I spent a lot of time trying to be Diana Ross."

In 1989 *TV Guide* put Oprah on the cover, using her face on the body of Ann-Margret. Oprah was shocked and hurt when she found out:

"This is the most embarrassing thing I can imagine. Just about everybody in the whole country will see that picture. I thought I looked pretty decent, but I guess the real me isn't good enough for *TV Guide*. The whole thing stinks."

She told an insider:

"Under different circumstances I would probably be delighted to switch bodies with Ann-Margret, but not to sell magazines. This cover is exploitive of women and personally humiliating to me.

"They wouldn't picture Phil Donahue on the body of Arnold Schwarzenegger. Just like him, I deserve to be treated with dignity."

In 1990 one of Oprah's new ABC projects was "In the Name of Self-esteem":

"Every show I do tries to encourage self-esteem. If we've got that, we've got it all.

"What we are trying to tackle in this one hour is what I think is the root of all the problems in the world—lack of self-esteem is what causes wars because people who really love themselves don't go out and try to fight other people. . . . It's the root of all the problems."

"All these years I have done show after show about low self-esteem, but because I was on TV, was famous, was making pots of money, I never thought I might be talking about me. In truth I was in denial about the problem despite all the signs of it.

"I didn't receive love as well as I give it. Actually I don't receive anything as well as I give it. Which is true of most people suffering with low self-esteem. We don't think of ourselves as worthy of receiving."

1992

In 1992 she was unable to take an extended vacation, she could not relax:

"I felt compelled to read, to do something that made me feel productive. I discovered I didn't feel worth a damn, and certainly not worthy of love, unless I was accomplishing something. I suddenly realized I have never felt I could be loved just for being."

"In your twenties and thirties you are always struggling to be open to what other people see as their vision of you. But you reach the point where you're not willing to accept the bull that you used to.

"I don't feel the pressure now to make sure people like me. Because I feel like I like me pretty much. And I'm forty, so if you don't, that's okay."

"This need to please has been the central theme and issue of my life. It is what was underneath the eating all those years. It is why I was abused."

1994

"I can be impossible to live with because I am so controlling."

Referring to 1994, which included a loss of almost eighty pounds:

"I would say 1994 was a time of profound change for me, emotionally, spiritually, and physically."

"People think because you're on TV, you have the world by a string. But I have struggled with my own self-value for many, many years."

"I allow myself to be vulnerable. It's not something I do consciously. But I am. It just happens that way. I'm vulnerable and people say, 'Poor thing. She has big hips too.' "

"I'm really no different from all of those women who are watching, because I want the same things for my life that they want. I want to be happy, a sense of fulfillment, children who love me, respect from my husband."

"All of my friends are thinner. And I tell you what, one of the reasons is because when I see other people who are overweight, I understand, spiritually, we all mirror each other, and I see them as people who are heavier than me, and I say, 'Oh, God, that could be me, that could be me.' And there is this fear that it might happen to me."

"I'm a born ham! You give me three people—and I'm *on*! Having an audience makes for a better day."

"I'm very secure. That's misinterpreted as arrogance, but not by anyone who knows me. I only play by my rules. I'm ruled by my own inner voice."

"You really can't afford to be anything else but be yourself, after all. Even if people don't like the subject or are not particularly interested in the subject, if you just always remain yourself or are able to tap into whatever it is about yourself that you can allow to be seen on camera, it works so much better."

"This is what I've found to be a truth. The more I am able to be myself, the more honest and open I am, the more honest and open my guests and audience tend to be. I don't hold anything back and therefore they don't. I take issue with people in this business who pretend they are like everybody else. I certainly know what it's like not to be able to pay the mortgage, but I don't pretend now that I can't afford leather boots. I don't like pretending. I've said, when we have fashion shows, that I have spent eight hundred dollars on a dress, and it causes a lot of resentment. And I've said, 'I'm thankful to you all for helping me to become what I am, which is a rich woman.' Other people in this business don't run into my problems because they don't let any of themselves out. You never know what they can or can't afford because they never tell you."

1986

"I have never felt a moment of guilt about what I have."

"For the most part, I like people. But my head hurts when I have to be in any situation where people are being phony. So if I can't be myself and take my shoes off when my feet hurt, then I'm not going to do very well."

A *Newsweek* article, combined with the *Tonight Show* appearance, prompted P. J. Bednarsky to ask Oprah, in the *Chicago Sun-Times*, if she might be getting "too big for her britches":

"I can tell you I'm more than a little offended by the question.... Anyone who knows me knows that can't happen to me. I'm offended by the whole 'la-di-dah, chi-chi, poo-poo' syndrome. I mean, it offends me. I think the reason people say that is they know if they got this much attention, they'd be crazy."

Paraphrased from Oprah's April 24, 1995, show, when she addressed the subject of the *Essence* magazine Twenty-fifth Anniversary cover:

"I want to stamp out a rumor: Apparently some people thought I looked too good to be for real. The head looks bigger because the rest of my body is in soft focus. It really is my body. It's the truth. I will always tell you the truth."

Outlook on Life

"I firmly believe that none of us in this world have made it until the least among us have made it."

"It is easier to go with the river than to try to swim upstream. Anything negative that happens to me is because I have been fighting against the stream."

"To those of us that much is given, much is expected."

She told a reporter that she had developed a respect for fish:

"Because I live my life in a fishbowl. I know how it is, guys. I won't even look in fishbowls anymore. I think, 'They must get sick of people walking by looking at them.' "

Oprah Herself

She confessed that she had no master plan:

"I am a live-for-the-moment, do-the-best-you-can-do-this-day kind of person. I never think of what's going to happen a year from now, two years from now, five years from now. I don't know. I really only worry about today."

1990

Explaining what she meant in 1990 by the "slave mentality":

"You don't have to have laws that say, 'You can't come here or go sit there in that place,' in order to be a slave. The only thing that can free you is the belief that you can be free."

"Don't let a bad childhood stand in your way."

"My main concern about myself is whether I will live up to my potential. I still sense that the best is yet to be. . . . The more you praise and celebrate your life, the more there is in life to celebrate. The more you complain, the more you find fault, the more misery and fault you will have to find. I am so glad I did not have to wait until I was fifty-two to figure this out, to understand the law of cause and effect—that divine reciprocity, reaping what you sow, is the absolute truth."

"I have a lot of things to prove to myself. One is that I can live my life fearlessly."

"Doing the best at this moment puts you in the best place for the next moment."

"What I have learned in my life and in my work is that the more I am able to be myself, the more it enables other people to be themselves. That is why people tell me things on the air that they have not been able to tell their mother, their daughter, their brother."

"The more positive you are about your life, the more positive it will be. The more you complain, the more miserable you will be."

"Do what you want to do, when you want to do it . . . and not a moment sooner."

"You can't do it all yourself. Don't be afraid to rely on others to help you accomplish your goals."

"Don't follow in *my* footsteps. Initiate your own guidance. Often intuition will direct you. If it feels right, it's probably right."

"What I do every morning is I go to my window. I watch the sun come up and I center myself and try to touch the God light that I believe is in all of us. Some people call it prayer, some people call it meditation; I just call it centering up. I get boundless, boundless energy from that. If there happens to be a day when I don't do it, I find myself loose, misdirected. I try to approach every show as if I hadn't done it ever before."

"I'm one of those people who lives for the moment. If you concern yourself with what's going to happen a year from now, or five years from now, you defuse the moment. Whatever comes, comes. For this time I enjoy the ascent. I don't worry about anything except getting thinner thighs."

"If you don't give something back when you get, you don't keep."

"I understand my commonality with the human experience. We all want to be happy, we have sad times. If you have lived, you have overeaten at one period or another. I'm not afraid to show those feelings. I can say, 'Look, I have been there, I understand how it feels to be in love with somebody and not have him love you back.' People say, 'Doggone that Oprah, isn't she something?' But they don't realize sometimes that I'm just like them."

"I'll give you the shirt off my back as long as you don't ask for it."

"I try to move with the flow of life and not to dictate what life should be for me, but just let it flow. So there may be a husband and there may be children. There may not be. I will celebrate either course that life hands me."

Oprah told *Family Circle*:
    "I have faith that the people in Tulsa and Nashville and New York are the same as they are in Chicago."

"My friends would probably say I need to be more organized. But I say that, too. They would say I'm very unconventional. Some people don't know how to take me sometimes. But I'm honest. I really am. I do just what I feel and hope it works."

"I believe people must grow and change; they must, or they will shrivel up. Their souls will shrink. I hope always to be expanding my life, always to be expanding my thinking. I want to expand myself in all ways, except the physical."

1993

To Bill Zehme of *Spy* magazine:

"I intend to do and have it all. I want to have a movie career, a television career, a talk show career. So I will do movies for television and movies for the big screen, and I will have my talk show. I will have a wonderful life. I will continue to be fulfilled doing all of those things, because no one can tell me how to live my life. I believe in my own possibilities, so I can do whatever I feel I'm capable of doing. And I feel I can do it all.

"I am as grounded as anybody you'll ever meet. And very, very God-centered. I know who the hell I am! And you have to be responsible for yourself, you see. You get more by doing what comes naturally than you do by efforting to get things! I move with the flow and take life's cues. Let the universe handle the details."

"I wanted to be a fourth-grade teacher. And my goal was, at the time, I was going to be the best fourth-grade teacher there was. And I wanted to, like—I thought I'd be Teacher of the Year. So, I think in anybody's life if you strive for excellence—I remember being, like, sixteen or seventeen years old, and I heard Jesse Jackson at an assembly program say once that excellence is the best deterrent to racism or sexism. I sort of took that on as my motto. So whatever I ever did, I always wanted to try to be the best at it. And my intention always in my life is I always try to do whatever is going to be the best for other people. For many years I looked out for other people even more than I looked out for myself. So I think it's . . . intention. It's grace. It really is, a lot of it, just the grace of God."

"I believe that all of us are brought to the light by people in our lives. Nobody gets to be anywhere in their life, of any note or success, without some other people who bring you along."

"The calling is to use my life in such a way that it brings the highest level of humanity to myself and also to those people who are reached."

"I understand there are a lot of sick people in the world. I understand that many people are victimized, and some people certainly more horribly than I have been. But you have to be responsible for claiming your own victories, you really do. If you live in the past and allow the past to define who you are, then you never grow."

"I look at problems as opportunities and use every person, every incident, and every encounter as an opportunity to show a more loving part of myself."

"I am so grateful for my life. I wouldn't trade my life with anyone."

"I'm everywoman. I make no judgments. I allow my vulnerability to show through. People recognize when you are willing to be raw and truthful, and it's a relief to have somebody not try to be perfect. They see themselves in me.

AWED (American Woman's Economic Development Corporation)

booked Oprah as keynote speaker for its February 1989 conference. She outlined her Ten Commandments for a successful life:

"1. *Don't live your life to please other people.*

"2. *Don't depend on externals to help you get ahead.*

"3. *Strive for the greatest possible harmony and compassion in your business and your life.*

"4. *Get rid of all the back stabbers around you.*

"5. *Be nice, not catty.*

"6. *Get rid of your addictions.*

"7. *Surround yourself with people who are as good or better than you are.*

"8. *If you're in it to make money, forget it.*

"9. *Never give up your power to another person.*

"10. *Don't give up.*"

Faith

~~~

"I have survived because of my faith in a power that is greater than me. In your moment of darkest pain, you know that you will be all right. Hopelessness is not believing that there is a way out. I have always been hopeful."

From America Online, October 3, 1995, when asked, *Have you ever felt like just giving up?*

"Lots of times. Faith sustains me, though. Faith that, no matter what, no matter how difficult life becomes, I'll be okay."

"I'm truly blessed. But I also believe that you tend to create your own blessings. You have to prepare yourself so that when opportunity comes, you're ready. I think that the path of our spiritual involvement is the greatest journey we all take. And I think that is part of the reason why I am as successful as I have been, because success wasn't the goal. The process was. I wanted to do good work. I wanted to do well in my life."

"I believe that life is eternal. I believe that it takes on other forms. And I believe that there's so many different levels that the mind can't even hold it all. So I believe that, yes, life will continue."

"I believe that so much of my life is a part of my own karmic destiny and that I am where I am because of all the events in my life."

"I am guided by a higher calling. It's not so much a voice as it is a feeling. If it doesn't feel right to me, I don't do it."

"I am extremely spiritual. I've not gone into this before because it's personal, but faith is the core of my life."

God

"I really do think, for me . . . it's gonna be about what you gave. You had all of this and what were you able to give back? And that question only gets answered by me. I know everybody who's listening will say, 'I can tell you what to give.' That question gets answered by me. It's between me and my God. The God. It's not about what everybody else thinks I should be giving. It's how you feel fulfilled within yourself. Did I do enough?"

"What I know is that God, nature, the Spirit, the universe, whatever title you wish to give him—or her—is always trying to help each one of us to be the best and do the best that we can."

"I know when this is all over, the Master isn't going to ask me how many things I owned."

"Once you understand God is the center of the universe, it's all very simple. Not a day goes by that I don't say, 'Thank you. I'm truly blessed.' "

"There is nothing greater than the spirit within you to overcome. You and God can conquer this. You can conquer it."

Asked if she ever feels God-like in the way she changes people's lives:
    "No! That's the only question you've asked I haven't liked. Because I am so connected to the bigger picture of what God is, I realize I'm just a particle in the God chain. I see God as the ocean, and I'm a cup of water from the ocean."

"A lot of people ask God for help and then wait for thunder and lightning. You have to be *receptive* enough to heed the call when it comes!"

"Every year I ask God for something. In 1994 it was clarity. But I also learned that you have to be careful what you ask for, because when you get it, the form may not be exactly what you had in mind. It may not be quite what you were expecting."

"Last year I asked God for freedom. Did I not come out of myself in a big way, breaking out of that fat shell? And this year I asked for clarity. I have become more clear about my purpose in television and this show."

"I would say 1994 was a time of profound change for me, emotionally, spiritually, and physically."

For Oprah the change wasn't all negative. There was her well-publicized loss of eighty pounds. But she also had to endure a drop in her ratings, trouble at Harpo Productions. including the resignation of executive producer Debra DiMaio, and a nasty lawsuit from her former publicist.

So Winfrey opted for a more conventional wish when she sat down for her chat with God for 1995:

"What I've asked God for this year is peace and a little joy. I was going to ask for wisdom. But I thought, no, I'll let another year pass before I ask for that, because I'm not sure I'm ready to see what will have to happen to bring me wisdom."

Prayer

"To this day I always say my prayers on my knees 'cause I think maybe they get there sooner."

"I pray every day. And I pray on my knees, like my grandma taught me."

"That's why it pays to be your best all the time, because you never know who's watching."

"I act as if everything depends upon me and pray as if everything depends upon God. Success in your work is not luck. If the door opens and you're not ready to go through . . . Acting, like poker, requires a great deal of skill, but you win or lose on how you apply good fortune."

"I always say my prayers at night on my knees. Stedman does, too."

"My prayer to God every morning on my knees is that the power in the universe should use my life as a vessel or a vehicle for its work.

"Prayer—that is the central thing for me. 'Use me so that everything I do, I do with this in mind.'

"That is my mission on the show, regardless of whether it is about learning to dance or about divorce or how to treat your children.

"The core for me is how to make people feel better about themselves."

"I have not missed a day in my life of praying. It's always about the same thing, using my life as a vehicle. Whatever I do, let it bring goodness to myself and to everybody that I come in contact with."

Spirituality

"People talk about spirituality like it's a very complicated thing. I don't think it is. I just try to listen to how I really feel. If something feels right,

I do it. If it feels wrong, I don't. It's really very, very simple, but you've got to be willing to take your chances doing stuff that may look crazy to other people—or not doing something that looks right to others but just feels wrong to you."

She had been fearful of what people would think when she took control of the show:

"So I went within, as I always do, and asked the Spirit: Is this the right thing for me to do? And the answer came back to me as a resounding yes! Then I asked the Spirit, 'Do you think I need a business course or something because my name ain't Iacocca?"

"As I got very firm with myself, I then understood that the best way to run a business is to do it the way you run your life."

1989

"It isn't until you come to a spiritual understanding of who you are—not necessarily a religious feeling, but deep down, the spirit within—that you can begin to take control."

"I think there is no life without a spiritual life. And I think that, more and more, people are becoming aware of the spiritual dynamics of life. And for me, it's always about, 'Why are you really here? What is your purpose really about? All the stuff that's really going on, what does it really mean?' I think that we've all just kind of gotten lost in believing that things of the exterior, all the things that we acquire, mean more."

"If you want to accomplish great things in your life, you have to begin with the Spirit. You have to go in and ask the Spirit if this is the right thing. 'Am I motivated for the right reason? Shall I take this road or that road?'

"The rules are simple—seek truth and follow the Spirit. I'm also convinced that the difference between how I handle my life and how some other people handle theirs is that I don't just pray. I truly heed the response I'm given. I listen to the voice of God within me. The times I haven't listened, I've gone ahead and made big mistakes."

Inspiration

Asked who has been her greatest inspiration other than the Creator:

"You're right—Creator's number one. And a whole series of people would be number two—with Mrs. Duncan, my fourth-grade teacher, leading the way. Maya Angelou of course. And everyday people who act with extraordinary courage."

SUCCESS

On *60 Minutes*, December 14, 1986:

"I was like a hit album waiting to be released. . . . I knew my day would come."

"These have been the best two years of my life. I swear, not a day goes by that I do not consciously say, 'Thank you. I'm truly blessed.'

"But I also believe that you tend to create your own blessings. You have to prepare yourself so that when opportunity comes, you're ready."

1986

During the *60 Minutes* interview with Mike Wallace, she explained her success:

"The reason I communicate with all these people is because I think I'm everywoman, and I've had every malady and I've been on every diet and I've had men who have done me wrong, honey. So I related to all of that. And I'm not afraid or ashamed to say it. So whatever is happening, if I can relate to it personally, I always do."

The success of *The Oprah Winfrey Show* made Oprah's thirty-sixth birthday on January 29, 1990, a sweet occasion:

"I wouldn't trade places with anybody. I'm growing up. And I think that I'm getting better because of it."

"You only have to believe you can succeed, that you can be whatever your heart desires, be willing to work for it, and you can have it."

"Don't be satisfied with just one success—and don't give up after failure."

"Ain't it something? Really. I mean, there are some days when I'm thinking, 'If it gets any better, I may just go jump over the moon.' "

1986

"It feels very good. Everything has its time and place. I look upon it as part of a process. I've been warming up for a long time. I've been in broadcasting since I was seventeen. I tell people, 'You are responsible for your own life.' I take full responsibility for my successes and failures, from getting up and getting my own talk show to losing my luggage on a trip."

"The whole path to success is not as difficult as some people would want you to believe. The process was the goal. I've taken great joy in the process. My main concern about myself now is whether I will live up to my potential; I already reach more people than many politicians ever do."

"I think, you know, what's so—so important to me is that God isn't a he or a she but is everything. I think that the path to our spiritual evolvement is the greatest journey we all take, and that—I think that's part of the reason why I am as successful as I have been, because the success wasn't the goal, the process was. I wanted to do good work. I wanted to do well in my life."

Money

~~~

"Before, if I couldn't decide which of two dresses I wanted, I bought them both. Now if I don't have the cash, I don't buy it. And when you have to count out five hundred dollars in bills, it makes you stop and think."

1986

"I knew I'd be a millionaire by age thirty-two. In fact I am going to be the richest black woman in America."

1987

"I have only allotted myself to personally only spend a million dollars this year. That's how much I'm giving myself to play with. I can do that without worrying if this ends, will I have enough to eat."

1987

"This is the glorious thing about finally getting money. When you finally get it, you realize it has its place."

1988

Asked about money—if it troubles her to have so much:
    "I'm rather amused by it. I just read forty million the other day and I said, 'Oooh, got a raise.' Now, it doesn't because my life really isn't defined by money. And it's easy to say when you have it and it's difficult to explain to people who don't have it that it's very nice and it's comfortable and it's nice, but it isn't what you think it is."

"I'm blessed with more money than I could ever use. I'm lucky. Life's short and I'm going to enjoy every minute of it!"

1990

"I live way below my means."

On buying sheets without waiting for the white sales:
"I didn't wait until somebody came to visit. I put them on the bed in the middle of the week."

In 1991, speaking of her work against child abuse:
"I used to write checks all the time. And I make decisions to give money based on my gut, like I make all other decisions in my life. I'm an instinct player and I still write a lot of checks. That's the easiest thing somebody like me can do, I think, is write a check."

It took time to get used to having all that money. A friend recalls going shopping for silverware. Oprah fretted over the choices, then realized that she could afford anything she wanted:
"We stopped dead in the street and I said, 'I can get both!' We starting jumping up and down and screaming."

Asked if she's happy:
"Are you kidding? Do you know how much money I made last year?"

1993

On being rich:
"I love it. I'm not going to lie. It's great! But I never thought it would

reach these proportions. I mean, I'd gone through syndication once before, back in Baltimore, and I got something like a ten-thousand-dollar increase in my salary. So that's what syndication success meant to me. I was thinking, 'Hey, maybe I'll get an extra ten thousand dollars this year.' Who could have foreseen this?"

"My fortune gives me choices. If a child is in need, I help. My money enables me to make an important difference in people's lives."

1994

"Money just *falls* off me. I mean it *falls* off!"

"I'm very generous, and yes, I give great presents. I mean, I'd love to get a present from me. This past Christmas, I gave trips anywhere in the world, pick the place on the map that you most want to go to."

"I don't feel I owe anybody anything. But my mother feels I do, so I'm buying her a house in Milwaukee. Maybe I feel guilty because I'm such an independent being. I'm hearing from so many people now who want me to give them money, or lend them money. . . . I called up my father and said, 'Dad, I'm a millionaire! I want to send you and your friends to any place in the world you want to go.' And he said, 'All I want is some new tires for my truck.' I was so upset!"

1986

From a *Good Housekeeping*, October 1995, interview with Liz Smith, when asked, *You give away a lot of money, which is a very interesting thing about you:*
   "At the end of every year they tell me how much I give to charity. But

there's a lot I give that nobody knows about. I gave money to people in Oklahoma after the bombing, and I told them not to tell anybody, because I couldn't give money to the entire state of Oklahoma. These were people I met personally who were going to be out of work for a while, and people who had lost family members.

"I have a new program where I'm taking a hundred families out of the projects that's going to cost me millions of dollars. But it's not the money that's most significant. I really believe I can change the way people who have been on welfare all of their lives think about themselves. It's taken me six months to find ten families to work with. I was at one family's house and I was talking to a thirteen-year-old boy who said he'd been late for school a lot. I said, 'Well, what's the matter? Your alarm clock doesn't work?' He said 'No, we don't have an alarm clock.' I said, 'So how do you wake up in the morning?' He said 'I just keep trying to wake myself up.' I bought the family an alarm clock. Nobody was making it to work or school on time because the concept of getting a clock had not entered their minds. They said, 'We just try. We're gonna try to wake up earlier tomorrow.' "

Power

"I'm finally ready to own my own power, to say, 'All right, this is who I am. If you like it, you like it. And if you don't, you don't. So watch out. I'm gonna fly.' "

"When you have an opportunity to reach millions of people and people listen to what you say, what do you want to say to the world? How can you improve the world?"

"Women have that common bond when it comes to giving up power. I speak to a lot of women now, trying to get them to understand that each of us is responsible for herself. You can read that in books, but it isn't until you come to a spiritual understanding of who you are—not necessarily a religious feeling, but deep down, the spirit within—that you begin to take control."

"My mission is to use this position, power, and money to create opportunities for other people."

"I understand that nothing happens to you without your deserving it or creating it in some way for yourself.

   "I believe from the time you are born you are empowered with the ability to take responsibility for your life. And to understand that, I'm telling you, makes me joyous. You can allow yourself to be a victim, or you can be the kind of person who understands that you have to take charge. It gives me great joy to know that I have this much control over my life. It's like soaring over the mountains."

"People have the power to make a difference in their lives."

On *This Morning*, May 20, 1992:
   "I attempt, in my life, in my relationships, in my work, and particularly on the show, to live it with the intention of empowering people and, because that is the intention, I think that is usually what happens."

"Unless you choose to do great things with it, it makes no difference how much you are rewarded or how much power you have."

"You have the power to make a difference in your life regardless of who you are or where you come from. You are responsible for yourself. It's what Alice Walker was saying in *The Color Purple:* You have the power; it starts right here with you."

CAUSES AND CONCERNS

Politics

During a promotional tour when her show was first syndicated nationally:

"It's like campaigning. It's given me a greater respect for candidates and what they go through. I think they ought to win based on how many cities they went to, not how many votes they get."

From *Good Housekeeping*, October 1995, when asked, *Do you intend someday to enter politics?*

"No. I think I could have a great influence in politics, and I think I could get elected. I'd have a fun campaign. But I think that what I do every day has far more impact."

"I've purposefully stayed away from politics. I'm only interested in presenting issues, so that I can allow people to see the truth for themselves. I've never been very good at interviewing political figures because I've never been able to penetrate their agenda to get to what I thought was the truth."

"It's a powerful medium [TV] . . . I think a politician would want to be me. If you really want to change people's lives, have an hour platform every day to go into their homes and say what you want to say."

When asked, *Do you vote?*

"Absolutely. I grew up reading black history, and I know how hard it was for us to get the vote. When I was young, a man named Otis Moss told me a story about his father, a black pastor, who had marched eighteen miles to vote the very first time. When he arrived, the poll was closed. He wasn't allowed to vote, and he died before the next election. Every Election Day I remind myself of Otis Moss's father and I go vote."

Children

In 1991 Oprah spoke before the Chicago Bar Association, which had invited her to participate in its Justice for Youth campaign:

"I really can think of no greater purpose in life than to be a voice for the children, the children who wish to be heard, but whose cries and wishes and hopes often fall upon deaf and inattentive ears."

She praised its work to transform the Cook County juvenile justice system:

"I'm really a spiritual person and I know that it is just spiritual law that you can't save a life without uplifting your own, and every time you remove a child from an abusive home, you rescue a child from neglect and emotional humiliation.

"Every time a child is saved from the dark side of life, every time one of us makes the effort to make a difference in a child's life, we add light and healing to our own lives.

"In my opinion we seem to have declared war against our children. The stories about abused children reveal a nation really at odds with itself."

On March 13, 1991, she devoted her program to child abuse:

"Our children in this country are not safe. They're not safe at the hands of strangers. Oftentimes they're not safe at the hands of relatives and friends and even their own parents. One of every six violent crimes in this country is committed against a child. And I think it's time for all of us to decide to do something about it."

From a *Good Housekeeping*, October 1995, interview with Liz Smith, when asked, *If you had the chance to change just one thing in the world, what would you do?*

"If I could change just one thing, I would stop people from beating their kids. Not just beating, but molesting, kids, verbally abusing kids, neglecting kids. The dishonor of children is the single worst problem in this country. If we ended it, there would be an incredible ripple effect on society. From the thousands of shows I've done over the past ten years, I see that the way people were treated as children causes them to grow up and behave in certain ways as adults. I see it as the root of almost every problem in our society.

"I think the most important job in the world is raising children. We have seen the toll taken on our children in this generation, and the generation coming, of women and men not being there for their children."

"Well, if you call that politics . . . I don't. I call that knowing the difference between right and wrong. I find that we pay a great deal of lip service in this country to the idea that 'children are our future.' But we don't put forward any programs that allow mothers to stay at home and look after their children, or allow women to work and know that their children are being taken care of in a safe environment. We just talk."

In her 1991 speech before the Chicago Bar Association Oprah said:

"I know what I'm talking about. I know it because I blamed myself for most of my adult life. You lose your childhood. People often say you lose your innocence, but I know you lose your childhood when you're abused.

"Jeff, my partner, and I have this saying, I say most people have a guardian angel, I have a team of guardian angels, and they've been working for me for a long time to bring blessings into my life. . . .

"I was, luckily, blessed that the system in Milwaukee, Wisconsin, in 1968 was already overworked and overcrowded before I was sent to a detention home. And it's very interesting. As I was preparing the words to say to you last night, it's the first time I thought about it.

"I've said many times before that I was raped when I was nine years old by a nineteen-year-old cousin, and then repeatedly sexually molested for the next five years after that.

"So by the time I was fourteen, I was really, really in the throes of acting out the abuse in other negative ways. I was, as my mother used to say, 'runnin' the streets.' I ran away a couple of times. I didn't want to be at home.

"I was literally looking for love in all the wrong places and getting myself deeper and deeper in trouble.

"And my mother, who was on welfare and had two other children at the time, didn't know what to do. She had no parenting skills. So her only alternative, she thought, was to put me in a detention home for girls.

"I knew I wasn't a bad person and I remember thinking how did this happen? How did I get here?"

"Children cannot stand alone; none of us do. There's not a one of us in this room, no matter how smart we are. . . . No matter how diligent or persistent you have been, there is not a one of us who made this journey toward success by ourselves.

"Somebody helped you; somebody helped me, and we have to help the children. We have to make the system better.

"Nothing, I don't know of one thing that angers me more in this world than hearing the story of a child being abused or assaulted or raped or murdered by someone who had a previous conviction for child abuse and then got out. Plea-bargained. Served eight months, was released, and came out to molest and murder another child."

THE NATIONAL CHILD PROTECTION ACT

The death of Angelica Mena, a four-year-old Chicago girl who had been molested, strangled, and thrown into Lake Michigan by Michael Howard, who had been convicted twice before of abducting and raping children, set Oprah in motion when she saw reports on the news in February 1991:

"I didn't know the child, never heard her laughter. But I vowed that night to do something, to take a stand for the children of this country."

She hired former Illinois governor James Thompson and the law firm of Winston and Strawn to draft legislation to create a national database of convicted child abusers (the National Child Protection Act of 1991):

"And if the bill is passed, and one child is spared, I'll be grateful. I know that children cannot stand alone. Children cannot stand alone, so I ask you, will you take a stand for the children or will you turn your back as you often do, knowing I'm your sons and I'm your daughters, too?"

"I hired the law firm of Winston, Strawn, and former governor James Thompson . . . because I figured that, because he has been the governor, he certainly knows about legislative proposals . . . and we, all together, put together this proposal and went to the Senate."

"I wept for Angelica, and I wept for us, a society that apparently cares so little about its children that it would allow a man with two previous convictions for kidnapping and rape of children to go free after serving only seven years of a fifteen-year sentence."

The bill would create an FBI-administered computer database available to schools and employers to check on the child-abuse histories of applicants for positions working with or caring for children. She said she would sponsor laws requiring mandatory sentencing of child abusers:

"We have to demonstrate that we value our children enough to say that when you hurt a child, this is what happens to you. It's not negotiable."

"I am committed to using all of my will to follow through on this legislation and on the issue of child abuse. I intend to make this my second career."

She was shown on *This Morning* on November 14, 1991, speaking on Capitol Hill about the National Child Protection Act:

"What I hope that it will do is prevent those people who have committed crimes against children and are then convicted of committing crimes against children—it will prevent them from having access, through employment, to children by allowing child-care organizations, including voluntary groups, to be able to check backgrounds of potential employees to make sure that there have been no crimes or offenses against children in their backgrounds. That's what I'm hoping."

She appeared before the Senate Judiciary Committee in 1991:

"This is my first effort at the federal legislative level to help protect children from child abuse. . . . I will lobby and work on this issue with the same energy I devote to my television career, and the Congress of the United States and the legislatures of the fifty states will be hearing from me."

Oprah went to Washington to push the National Child Protection Act. It required states to register names and Social Security numbers and other information about anyone convicted of child molestation and report it to the U.S. Justice Department. The information becomes available via the FBI to employers screening job applicants for positions working with children:

"Pedophiles seek employment where they will be in contact with children. There are millions upon millions of silent victims in this country that have been and will continue to be irrevocably harmed unless we do something to stem this horrible tide."

"I believe this bill will be passed. I'm going back to Washington next week to—or in the next coming weeks to meet with some members of the House and so forth. I believe this bill will be passed. But the truth of the matter is, I know and you know that this is just a start. It's a small start. I'm glad that I did something and I'm really glad for all the support of people who, since I appeared on Capitol Hill, have been calling our offices and, as I walk down the street, mothers come up to me saying, 'What can we do? What can we do?' What I really want to do, in the very near future, is to meet with various child-advocacy groups around the country who have been working on legislation and proposals."

On the *Today* show November 14, 1991:

"The proposed legislation won't help people who were in the same situation that I was in and the millions of other children who are being abused by family members and friends of the family, but what it will do, I hope, is prevent those people who have been convicted of offenses against children from having access to children. What it will do is require all states to report to a national registry so that if you are a child-care organization, even a voluntary one, you can check a registry to see if the people that you are trying to employ, who will be providing services to children, have some kind of criminal record or have criminal offenses against children. And then you can make the decision.

"That person can also decide that 'I don't want you to make the check' and make the decision not to be hired. That's to protect their own privacy. But it will be left up to the child-care organization to then check. We're not mandating or requiring that they do, but I think that a lot of child-care organizations want the ability to be able to find out about the people that they're hiring."

"As I said the other day while testifying before the Senate Judiciary Committee, this is a second career for me. I think there are a lot of people who have notoriety and become spokespeople and so forth, I don't intend just to be a figurehead. What I'm going to do is call a summit of all the various child-care organizations who have for years—because I'm really sort of a Johnny-come-lately to this—I'm just a person who has a name and some notoriety right now who can get some attention to this issue.

"But there are people who've been working for many, many years who have wanted legislation, who have some serious ideas about what should be done to protect children in this country. So I'm going to, in January, hold a summit of my own with all of these various leaders of organizations so that I can get information from them, just as I did from Andrew Vox, about what is the next step. What I really want to do, my ultimate goal, is to start a movement in this country to empower the children. Because many times when children—there are children, and I would have been one of those children, who would have told if I had felt that I was valued enough, important enough, or had felt that somebody would have listened."

"I think it's just a crime that in—in one state you can get five years for molesting or even killing a child, another state—you can get ten, another state you can plea-bargain, another state you can be paroled.

"I think that as a nation we say we care about children, and I think that as a nation, if we really do, we have to say if you molest a child, if you commit a crime against a child, we agree that there should be whatever years it is agreed upon for sentencing, that it shouldn't vary from state to state, it really should not. If you want to protect children, then you have to take a stand, I think."

"Why do we only talk about this on talk shows? Why isn't it part of the legislature?"

President Clinton signed the "Oprah Bill" against child abuse in 1993:

"I try to use the show as a voice—to try to make a difference in the lives of children, especially, and those who watch us."

The bill became law on December 20, 1993.

CHILD ALERT

In 1995 Oprah Winfrey launched Child Alert, a year-long campaign that each month addresses the challenges facing America's children. She believes the campaign "will at least move people to take some action. I want to raise the consciousness of America and, beyond that, get them to do something."

Why she focused on kids and guns:

"It's something we can change today. There's a whole lot I can't change. Racism? I can't change that anytime soon. Or the entire economic system. But you can turn in your gun tomorrow, and that could be the day your depressed teenager wants to commit suicide or take a gun to protect himself."

From an *Atlanta Journal* interview, October 30, 1995, when asked, *This is going to sound like talk-show-speak, but aren't guns a symptom of bigger problems?*

"The gun is the issue. How people handle the gun is the second phase. There are a lot of problem kids, and I'm not going to change what causes them to want to use the gun. But I can take the gun."

"There are just too many guns lying around that kids can get their hands on. There is no reason why fifteen children should be dying every day as a result of guns.

"I'm not taking on the NRA. This is voluntary. We've got to do something.

"Why are there 1.2 million children going home after school to homes where there are guns and no parental supervision?

"I want to put a face on the millions of children who are dying because of gun violence."

FAMILIES FOR A BETTER LIFE

"Money is an easy thing to give away. You know what I did that I am the most proud of for myself? You didn't ask, but I'm going to tell you. I started a program called Families for a Better Life."

After the filming of the TV movie *There Are No Children Here* in 1993, Oprah and Stedman founded Families for a Better Life, a nonprofit foundation, through which they plan to sponsor one hundred families, helping them obtain jobs, counseling, and homes outside the projects:

"It's a war zone. We have to get them out. We're giving them bootstraps."

"What I think I'm giving is a sense of a belief in themselves, for people to believe in themselves. To take families out of the projects and get families jobs and get families working and work with them on a one-on-one basis so that you can break the cycle of poverty, that's the most important thing, because you can . . . buy anybody a house. I've done it—you know, I've done it in my own family. Buying a house doesn't mean anything. It is how you change the way people think. Breaking the cycle of victimization is what I'm trying to do."

"I think if you can do that a hundred times over, then you will really have done something. This way people learn to support themselves."

From America Online, October 3, 1995, when asked, *I recently heard about your plan to take a few families out of the projects:*

"My goal is to take a hundred. Each family has to go through a training program because there's a process to success, I believe. You can't just give a family a house and expect them to be successful. You have to teach them responsibility. So that's what the training program's about. So far, eight families have been through. Ten more start next month. It's a slow process, but we're dealing with people's lives. It's like having foster families for me—with all the joys and problems that come with that."

"Stedman was the catalyst for this. He is a systems man and I was inspired by his guidance. And on this project together, it's like we sing. We just really sing."

Race and Racism

On her blackness she divides her race into "fudge brownies," "gingerbreads," and "vanilla creams":
"I'm a fudge. No one's ever going to mistake me for anything else."

"The vanilla creams are the girls who could pass if they wanted to. I mean, they're sort of borderline. Gingerbreads are the girls who, even though you know they're black, have all the features of white women—the lips, the nose, maybe even a green eye here and there.

"The fudges? No doubt about it. We are black women. You will never see *me* and say, 'Gee, I wonder if she's mixed. I wonder if she's Puerto Rican.' You say, '*There*—now, *there*—is a black woman.'

"In society, as little black children, we were taught that the browner you were, the tougher time you were going to have in life. So a lot of little blacks are born and their parents look at them and say, 'We'll educate her.' That's what they did with me!

"There was another black college [not Tennessee State University] where *all* the vanilla creams went. I thought it was a better school, but I wouldn't go, just because I didn't want to have to compete with the vanilla creams, because they always got the guys."

" 'Excellence is the best deterrent to racism.' I was already working in television at the time, and I believed that the struggle had taken a new direction, and that was for us to be the best, to make the most of the doors that had been opened."

One of her most provocative shows was one aired from Cumming in Forsyth County, Georgia, site of civil rights demonstrations:

"You are looking at land in America where not a single black person has lived in seventy-five years. We watched as thousands in this town marched to shouts of 'Nigger, go home.' We came here today not to argue whether black people have a right to be here—the Civil Rights Act guaranteed them that right—we are here to try to understand the attitudes and motivations of those who threw rocks at the recent demonstrations."

1987

She once interviewed the Grand Dragon of the Ku Klux Klan:

"It was as if the burden of every black person was on my back."

She identifies herself first as a woman, then as a black woman:

"Whenever I hear the words *community organization* or *task force*, I know I'm in deep trouble. People feel you have to lead a civil rights movement every day of your life, that you have to be a spokeswoman and represent the race. I understand what they're talking about, but you don't have to do it, don't have to do what other people want you to do. Blackness is something I just am. I'm black. I'm a woman. I wear a size-ten shoe. It's all the same to me."

"There are still a lot of black people who are very angry and bitter. They want me to be just as angry and bitter, and I won't be. It just burns me. Some black people say I'm not black enough. I wonder, how black do you have to be? The drums of Africa still beat in my heart, and they will not rest until every black boy and every black girl has had a chance to prove their worth."

Asked if she's hurt by being called an "Oreo" or accused of pandering to whites, and so on:

"I used to be very hurt by it and I used to always think that I had to defend it and always make people know that, yes, I really am black and I really am proud of it, and no, I'm not an Oreo at all. I don't feel that anymore because I know in my spirit that I care about what happens to black people and people in this country."

1988

Asked if she ever wished she were white:

"As a little girl I wanted to be . . . and it's the kind of thing I hesitate to say because when you say it, all the black groups call you and say, 'How dare you say it,' but, yes, I did. Now I understand, not because white is better, but because, in my mind, the white kids were loved more. They received more. Their parents were nicer to them. So I wanted that kind of life. . . . You know what changed it for me? The night I saw Diana Ross and the Supremes on *The Ed Sullivan Show*. I thought, 'I want to be like that.' . . . There are so many little pieces to the process that have helped me to be who I am. It's something as small as seeing Diana Ross and the Supremes. I remember the night I was ten years old and Sidney Poitier received the Academy Award for *Lilies of the Field*. And I thought to myself, 'I'm going to be there.' It makes me want to cry because it was the first time I thought, 'I can do that.' So the night I was at the Academy Awards, I just thought, 'I did this.' "

"I transcend race, really. I believe that I have a higher calling. What I do goes beyond the realm of everyday parameters. I am profoundly effective. I know people really, really *love* me, *love* me, *love* me. A bonding of the human spirit takes place. Being able to lift a whole consciousness—that's what I do."

"Most people out there have no contact with black people ever. Their only images are the ones portrayed on television. There's a whole reality outside of what most people know, where the black community functions on its own, where people own businesses, where people care about their property and their children and pay their taxes. The point of having your own company is that you can show that."

"I was told before I moved here that Chicago was a racist city and I'd be miserable. But I have never experienced that. I do find racism to be a reality. But I haven't personally experienced it. Because people treat you differently when you are famous and have money. They are *always* happy to see you."

"The greatest responsibility I feel is to my Creator, and what I try to fulfill for myself is to honor the creation. The fact that I was created a black woman in this lifetime, everything in my life is built around honoring that. I feel a sense of reverence to that. I hold it sacred. And so I am always asking the question, 'What do I owe in service having been created a black woman?'"

From *USA Today*, January 23, 1995:
    "I never forget who I am, and I am a black woman. I know people say I'm 'colorless' because of the popularity, but that's totally wrong. Wherever I go, whenever I enter a place or a store or a whatever, I know that they know here comes a black woman. Color is always a factor in this country."

One of Chicago's ritziest department stores once barred her from entering:
    "They didn't recognize me because I was wearing my hair all kind of . . . [an airy gesture suggesting a mega bouffant]. I was with my hairdresser, a black man, and the excuses they gave were . . . interesting.
    "They hummed and they hummed and they hummed, and then they said they'd been robbed the week before by two black transvestites!
    " 'Oh thank you very much,' I said. . . . 'OmyGad,' I said, 'I'm changing my hairdo!'

"Then I turned to my hairdresser and said, 'I think we are experiencing a racial moment.' At first you can't even believe that it's happening to you. 'So this is what it's like. Oh, man!' "

"I was standing in a drugstore, waiting in line for service. The girl was on the phone talking to her boyfriend. Now, if Oprah Winfrey had walked into the pharmacy, the girl would've gotten off the phone. But I was just another black woman. A black woman in braids. I had to ask three times, 'Which way is the aisle?' I never said anything and I never went back. I just thought, 'Yes. She's treating me like a second-class citizen.' "

"I think you never go beyond color. I think—and I never forget that no matter how much money I have, how much so-called power, how many people say I'm powerful, that when I walk into a supermarket, the first thing that they see is a black woman."

On apartheid:
  "It is a black holocaust to me."

Some black people criticize Oprah despite her success:
  "I hear this. I hear this a lot. I hear that I don't hug the black people the way I hug the white people, that I go to the white people in the audience first. First of all, there are *more* white people. There just are more! I could not survive with this show if I only catered to black people. I just could not! I couldn't be where I am if I did. That's not what it's about!"

"Some people say, 'Oprah, you're not black enough. You don't do enough interviews with blacks, you hug more whites than blacks, you get more white people in the audience.' I tell them I look for the best possible guest, someone who can add to the conversation, someone who's articulate, but I can't say, 'You can turn on the set every day and see black people on my show.' For us to transcend race, sexual bias, and hatred in Chicago, the most racist city in the country, is really something. I would get phone-ins from white people who would say, 'Oprah, we love you, we watch you every day, but don't come around our neighborhood.' "

SHORT SUBJECTS

Addiction

"Having been a food addict, I can identify with the woman who is an alcoholic. . . . I really, really understand people's pain. I understand it at a level that the people on the show many times don't even know that I understand it. What they do see is that because I have been so open, so exposed, so vulnerable, that I might understand. I might."

1993

Aging

In January 1987 Oprah turned thirty-three:

"It's a glorious time for me. I'm doing exactly what I wanted to be doing at age thirty-three. I feel I'm ripening, coming into my own. It's an exciting time, an exciting age."

On the occasion of her fortieth birthday:

"Oh, boy, am I looking forward to it. Quincy Jones once told me that after you're forty, you really just don't care anymore what people think. And I am so looking forward to that."

"I'm deliriously happy. If I get any happier, I may die. I think: 'Am I gonna die soon or what?'"

AIDS

In 1989 her half brother, Jeffrey Lee, died of AIDS at twenty-nine:

"For the last two years my brother, Jeffrey Lee, had been living with AIDS. My family, like thousands of others throughout the world, grieves not just for the death of one young man but for the many unfulfilled dreams and accomplishments that society has been denied because of AIDS."

In December 1988 colleague Billy Rizzo was dying of AIDS:

"I love Billy like a brother. He's a wonderful, funny, talented guy, and it's just heartbreaking to see him so ill."

"When things weren't going right for me, when my heart was sinking, I always had Billy to cheer me up. He'd always lend me his shoulder to cry on. I have all the money in the world and I can't help one of my dearest friends."

Oprah responds to a critical (and homophobic) audience member (in reference to AIDS):

"Isn't that why not enough is being done to find a cure, because of judgments such as yours?"

Anger

"What I understand is, anger doesn't do anything but destroy. It isn't even that I forgive him [her abuser]. I haven't forgiven him. It doesn't matter to me. I know that won't happen to me again, and if I have children, I will prepare them so that it doesn't happen to them. How? I will have the kind of relationship with my child that that child will feel free to tell me anything."

1986

"My biggest fault is that I do not express anger very well. What I've learned about being angry with people is that it generally hurts you more than it hurts them. All the anger that you're trying to vent breeds so much frustration."

Beauty

She appeared in a 1989 photo composite for Revlon's Most Unforgettable Women in the World ads:

"As a child it never occurred to me I might be considered beautiful, being none of the models looked like me.

"If just one little black girl sees the photo and thinks she's beautiful because she sees a part of herself in me, I will be grateful."

She donated her fee to inner-city schools.

On being told she is pretty:
"It's a compliment I can't take."

Books

"Books showed me there were possibilities in life, that there were actually people like me living in a world I could not only aspire to but attain. Reading gave me hope. For me it was the open door."

In 1991 she donated $100,000 for the new Harold Washington Library in Chicago:
"Books were my path to personal freedom. I learned to read at age three and soon discovered there was a whole world to conquer that went beyond our farm in Mississippi."

Her favorite books:
"*Their Eyes Were Watching God* by Zora Neale Hurston, and *To Kill a Mockingbird* by Harper Lee."

Short Subjects

Business

In 1993, speaking of her business ability:

"I don't do anything unless it feels good. I don't move on logic. I move on my gut. And I have a good gut."

From *TV Guide*, January 7-13, 1995:

"I used to always say, 'I never went to business school and I've never read a business book.' But now I think maybe I should have read a few."

Depression

Stephen Arterburn, author of *Hand-Me-Down Genes and Second-Hand Emotions* helped her understand that she was suffering from depression during her days in Baltimore:

"We were all talking [about depression], and somebody says, 'Well, you know, when you were sexually abused, weren't you depressed?' I said, 'I don't know if I was or not.' I do remember going through a period in my twenties when I thought I was in love, but I really was just obsessed. All I would do was live for this man. And if a man wasn't around, then I was in bed . . . waiting. Couldn't get myself out of bed. But was that depression or was I just crazy?"

Short Subjects

Education
꘡

One of her favorite audiences is still underprivileged teenagers. She has been known to tell them:

"I was like a lot of you. I was a hot little mama."

"The biggest thing I tell them is that you cannot do anything without an education. In this country, at this particular time, we happen to be speaking the King's English. At some other time, maybe, we will change to another language. But right now it's the King's English. If you are not able to do that, you are already ten paces behind."

From America Online, October 3, 1995, when asked, *Oprah, you are a hero of some sorts to many people. Do you feel that this has a great impact on your life?*

"Not really. If I wasn't doing this, I'd be teaching fourth grade. I'd be the same person I always wanted to be, the greatest fourth grade teacher and win the Teacher of the Year award. But I'll settle for twenty-three Emmys and the opportunity to speak to millions of people each day and, hopefully, teach some of them."

1995

Failure
꘡

She told the graduating class of Spelman College, 1993:

"Think like a queen. A queen is not afraid to fail. Failure is another stepping-stone to greatness."

"I will tell you that there have been no failures in my life. I don't want to sound like some metaphysical queen, but there have been no failures. There have been some tremendous lessons."

Fears

"I have a fear of being disliked, even by people I dislike."

1986

To her studio audience:
  "How many women here today are on the pill?"

Oprah admits that she uses birth control pills, and that she's afraid of facing menopause:
  "Terrified! Does anyone else feel that way?"

Greatness

"What I want to tell you is that I believe all of us have the potential for greatness in our lives. Greatness does not necessarily mean being famous or being well known, but if you allow yourself to seek greatness in your life, you will be known for doing great things."

"Somewhere I have always known that I was born for greatness in my life. Somewhere I've always felt—I remember being on my grand-mother's farm and knowing at four years old. I just always knew, just always knew. I don't regret being born illegitimately and living part of my life with my grandmother and part with my father, my mother. I don't . . . regret all of that past confusion. I don't regret it at all. It has made me exactly who I am."

From a *Good Housekeeping*, October 1995, interview with Liz Smith, when asked, *Once you said to Barbara Walters, "All my life I have always known I was born to greatness"*:
"Yes, Barbara had a pillow done for me with that quote on it. I've paid for that comment for many years in the press. I had read one of Martin Luther King's books in which he talked about greatness coming from service, and that's what I was referring to. I remember standing on the back porch of our little shotgun house as a child watching my grandmother boil clothes in one of those big, black iron pots—stirring them with the stick. I remember knowing inside that my life would be much bigger than that. I wasn't in school yet, I had not seen life or even television. But I knew that there were greater things ahead for me—that somehow I would be able to speak to people. I always thought I was going to be a preacher or a teacher or a civil rights leader. Now I see my TV show as a great forum for teaching. It's the biggest class-room you could ever imagine."

Heritage

In her speeches her pride in her heritage is reflected:

"My name is Oprah. Not Opree, nor Okree, and definitely not Okra. I consider myself one black woman, one voice. I was born in Kosciusko, Mississippi, around the corner from the Nile and down the street from Kenya. The drums of Africa still beat in my heart."

"I have a great sense of heritage. I feel a strong sense of legacy. But I'm not a flag-waving activist. I think excellence is the deterrent to racism. It's tough to convince others of that. I wanted to be part of the brother-sister network. I wanted to be nice, to be liked. If I thought somebody didn't like me, I was shattered."

"I live my life in such a way that I think the ancestors would be proud. And you know it all sounds rhetorical and lofty, but that's really how I try to lead my life.

"The ancestors don't deserve the treatment that we're giving them. They don't deserve it, and I believe that. I see us as a people doing things to ourselves and our children. I see the drug problem. I see abusiveness toward ourselves.

"I see self-hatred that makes us turn against each other and try to pull each other down. I see that and I think that Frederick Douglass did not deserve this. He did not teach the slaves to read by candlelight to see us at our banquets and meeting halls sit and try and tear each other apart. He does not deserve this.

"Your grandmother and great-grandmother did not work in the white folks' kitchen just trying to make enough money so that your mother might be able to have a pair of shoes to wear to school and not be embarrassed. They don't deserve great-grandchildren who don't take books to school. They don't deserve it."

On December 4, 1989, she was mistress of ceremonies for the Forty-fourth National Convention of the National Council of Negro Women at the Washington Hilton's Crystal Ballroom:

"I come here tonight celebrating not only the finalists and the honorees and the rest of us gathered here in this room, but I come here celebrating every African, every colored, black, Negro American everywhere that ever cooked a meal, ever raised a child, ever worked in the fields, ever went to school, ever sang in a choir, ever loved a man or loved a woman, every cornrowed, every Afroed, every wig-wearing, pigtailed, weave-wearing one of us.

"I come celebrating the journey, I come celebrating the little passage, the movement of our women people. I include everybody because I believe that it is everybody's contribution that has allowed us to stand, that has allowed me to stand on solid rock here tonight at the Hilton Hotel."

Hope

"Everybody wants hope, whether you live in the projects or downtown."

"People in the projects are no different from people everywhere. You can live in the projects and still want a life that's good and meaningful and be hopeful for your children."

Image

"You really have to work hard to let what you are come through."

"I hate being called fat."

1987

"People feel a real camaraderie to me. I don't pretend I'm something I'm not."

Her Life

"My schedule is very hectic, but it's exactly the kind of life I've always wanted. I've always said I wanted to be so busy that I wouldn't have time to breathe."

1987

"It's great. I'm happier than I've ever been, and healthier. So, of course, my first thought when I say that is, 'Okay, now when do I get hit by a truck?'"

1993

"There's no part of my life I regret—not even being fat."

"Life to me is all about evolving. But instead of slowly moving forward, as I do most years, I was sort of thrust forward last year."

1995

Luck

"Luck is a matter of preparation. I am highly attuned to my divine self."

1984

"Luck is a matter of preparation meeting opportunity."

Motherhood

Discussing single-parent families on her show:

"This happens in a lot of families where there's a single parent and the mother runs the family: There are boyfriends going in and out of the house, and daughters, particularly, see this. Mothers say, 'Don't let some man do this. You keep your dress down! You do what I say!' When what the child sees is entirely different from what the mother is saying.

"I had that when I was a kid. 'Do as I say, not what I do.' But that doesn't work. Doesn't work."

"The mothers who are home watching . . . those are my heroines. What it takes to do that. . . .One of my former producers, who worked for me for ten years, is now at home holding her baby, and she is there for every moment of that child's needs. To be able to create an environment that is stimulating, nurturing, teaching, a sense of moral values. What in the world is more important than that? The patience, the sacrifice . . . I don't have that."

Motivation

At times Oprah herself needs motivation. Playing LaJoe Mitchell in *There Are No Children Here* turned out to be painful:

"The story of her life is far more devastating than anything I could have imagined."

Oprah spoke of seeking inspiration from Troy, a youngster she had invited into her trailer for a pep talk after spotting him staring at her shyly from the sidelines:

"You've got what it takes to get out of here," she told the above-average student. "You can make it."

Her voice giving way to emotion, Oprah recalled:

"You should have seen him. His whole face lit up. . . . You can't save the world, but you can save a Troy."

From America Online, October 3, 1995, when asked, *What keeps you motivated?*

"To work or to work out? To work—it is a mission for me, this show, more than just a talk show. I want people to see things on our show that make them think differently about their lives. That make them better. For working out, my motivation is I don't want a fat butt!"

Poverty

"I recognize the problem with people who are in cyclical poverty is that they haven't learned to break the chain of poverty *for themselves*. You are taught to be a victim, and you can be taught not to be one."

"You can be born poor and black and female and make it to the top."

Psychiatry

Winfrey may speak like a woman who has spent a lot of time on a shrink's sofa—but she hasn't:

"Sometimes I wish I had. It would have been fascinating. I would have driven the therapist crazy. I'd have him on the couch saying, 'You think so?' "

"I'm beginning to think I'd have done myself a lot more good if I had been on a psychiatrist's couch all these years instead of doing my therapy on TV."

"I was so adamant about being my own person that I wouldn't go for counseling."

"It would probably take years of therapy to figure it out. Sitting here at forty, I think that what I did was repress whatever it was that I was feeling, blamed myself, and tried to cover up by pleasing some more. The abuse was allowed to continue because of my desire to please."

Shopping

"I was in Kmart buying a rug to go on the front porch so when people wipe off their feet, and they had—you had a choice between ducks and kittens, or a little pond, or a little saying—'Welcome Friends,' or 'Home Sweet Home.' They were $5.95. I'm telling you, I must have spent an hour in that store. I had them all lined up, trying to make the right decision about, yeah, a $5.95 mat."

1991

"I don't find the excitement in it that I used to. There is not another thing, not a shoe, antique, outfit, that I need to buy. Last year it was real exciting when I went from a size twenty-four to a size eight. But now I've been eight for a while."

1994

Skiing

In 1990 she took up skiing:

"Skiing is the next best thing to having wings."

Theater

She told an audience at a black theater festival in Winston-Salem, North Carolina, that black theater had been instrumental in her rise to stardom. She watched Ruby Dee in *A Raisin in the Sun* when she was growing up in Mississippi:

"I let that vision carry me. If there had not been black theater, there would not be an *Oprah Winfrey Show*."

The Tonight Show

"Nothing is supposed to happen on *The Tonight Show* that you don't know is supposed to happen. They give you a script. They tell you what you're going to be asked, so you know ahead of time. You go over the script before you go on."

1985

With less than eight hours before her scheduled appearance, Oprah was still without a suitable pair of shoes to wear on the show. She wanted something to match the rhinestone-studded, blue suede gown she had commissioned a Chicago designer to create especially for her first *Tonight Show* appearance. As luck would have it, Oprah found just what she was looking for in a Rodeo Drive shop, a $750 pair of blue, rhinestone-studded shoes:

"I'm not an extravagant person. I went to L.A. and needed some blue suede shoes and couldn't find them. And I was up and down looking for them, too. It was three o'clock in the afternoon and I needed shoes. So I took the first ones I saw.

"I didn't want to sweat it out, so I padded around backstage in my stocking feet."

"I was so nervous. And I'm never nervous. I mean, I've done lots of things and I've never, ever been nervous. I've spoken before thousands and thousands of people and wasn't nervous. I introduced the Jacksons at the Jacksons' concert and wasn't nervous. But gee whiz, gee whiz. You think to yourself, 'My God! This is it! Here's the curtain! This is the curtain!' And I'm standing behind the curtain and a stagehand says to me, 'Don't worry, honey, I've seen the best of them throw up right here.' And I said, 'Don't you worry. I'm not gonna throw up!' "

After the show Oprah headed for Spago's:

"When they brought out this chocolate mousse raspberry cake and Quincy Jones started singing 'Happy Birthday' to me, I thought about that Michelob commercial and I said, 'It just doesn't get any better than this.' "

Travels With Oprah

ETHIOPIA

Oprah went to Ethiopia to host a documentary for WLS-TV in Chicago. The station had participated in the famine relief fund and wanted to show viewers where the money was going:

"I think the devastation in Ethiopia transcends all that. I don't care what anybody says about that.

"You go there and you look very healthy, and you imagine, you're out in this desert with these people who look at you and think . . . what? 'Hi, I'm Oprah Winfrey and standing in front of me are five hundred Ethiopian children.' It's sick, isn't it?

"What I do understand is once you see it, nothing you've seen or read before will compare to it."

Oprah thought the trip would be a life-changing experience:

"The first time was when we first arrived in the city, because it's such a cultural shock. I mean, everybody is walking with donkeys and goats in the street, and there are children carrying eight pounds of wood on their backs to sell.

"They're beautiful children. And sometimes they grow up hump-backed because they've never learned to walk straight. That is their life and livelihood. Initially that was very upsetting.

"And there were these children who came running down from the hill carrying wood on their backs. They saw us and knew we were foreigners. 'For-en'gees,' they called us. It just broke my heart. I knew how myopic these children were, how limited. They don't know that there's another world out there. They don't even know.

"We were drinking these Cokes and we gave it to them. If you could've seen the smiles—from a Coca-Cola! It was an amazing thing. To say that you feel blessed is not even worth saying, at this point, because it's an understatement. Of course you're blessed. But the problem, then, is what do you do? What I understood on that hill is that, one at a time, we can make a difference. It sounds trite. But for some reason that thought occurred to me, that you really can. You can't take every child out of the hills of Ethiopia, but you can do what you can to make a difference.

"People say, 'Oh, gee, we have problems here. Why are you going over there?' But I really do think the problem of starvation and famine far exceeds anything. When you see children who have not bathed in years, who have only rags—and *rags* is not even the word—and the rags are infested with lice, it's an amazing thing.

"The basic human rights to food and shelter are denied. I mean, children freeze. Most of the people die between four and five in the morning because that's when its coldest in the desert. You die because there's not a blanket. So you understand a lot about the world and what matters and what doesn't.

"Although the people are being fed over there, they're fed and then they wait for their next feeding. They're fed again and then they wait again for their next feeding. What I understood was, unless you create a society in which people can take care of themselves and be responsible for themselves, then you really basically have no society. So what's the point? The point is to keep people from starving obviously. But the point also is to set up some kind of educational system so that people can better themselves. And you can only do that through knowledge. You just can't do that sitting on a hill weaving baskets.

"But it's a good Band-Aid because, without the rest of the world, without us, a people would've died. It's so clear. You understand that nobody else is doing anything—that the Ethiopian government is not, for whatever reasons, political and otherwise, so we really have made a difference."

EUROPE

"You order a salad in France and it comes in a *cream* sauce. I was in Paris this summer, but I came home early because I didn't like the food."

1994

"After a little over a week in Europe, I gave up and came back to Chicago because they don't know what low-fat food is."

1995

NEW YORK

"You know, it doesn't get any more real than New York."

Short Subjects

In 1989 Oprah confessed to Liz Smith that she was tired:

"I've been traveling recently and went through five time zones in five days. I was in London, France, L.A., Atlanta, Columbus, and Chicago. But I can't wait to get to New York."

"I feel overwhelmed, frustrated, and out of control in New York. I don't know what to do with myself. I go to New York for the weekend and I stay in the hotel and order Chinese food. I don't know where to go, or what to do, because there's too much and it makes me crazy. On several occasions we've been there, myself and the staff, and we end up in bed by nine. We're some party animals, I'll tell you, but I love Chicago."

OKLAHOMA CITY

Oprah said she had trouble sleeping through the night after she came back from Oklahoma City. She was there visiting injured children and their families at Children's Hospital. Oprah said that she became so emotional that

"one of the mothers was holding me up saying, 'You're going to be all right, Oprah.' "

At the bed of a badly burned four-year-old girl, Oprah said:

"I picked up her hand, and there was this little finger with nail polish on it. . . . And I just lost it."

When she got to the bed of Brandy Liggons, the last person pulled out alive, Oprah recalled:

"I said, 'Brandy, if you can hear me, I want you to know, you're the strongest woman I've ever known. . . . If you survived that, you can survive anything.' And she opened her eyes."

From *USA Today*, April 26, 1995, Oprah worried about how the families would cope:

"I cannot even imagine what it would be like to lose a child or a family member. I wonder, 'Will they ever sleep again?' "

SOUTH AFRICA

In 1995, asked about a trip to South Africa:

"It was beautiful, far more beautiful than I imagined. But also Alexandria—I saw some of the most devastating poverty."

WEST VIRGINIA

In 1995 Oprah visited two low-income families in West Virginia. She intended to avoid backwoods stereotypes:

"I'm a black female in America, so I understand how images of people create ideas about people."

"I picked West Virginia because I love it. I mean that song's always going through my head, 'Almost Heaven, West Virginia.'

"I just think it's so plush, and the state itself looks like it's filled with abundance, and yet so many times you find many people who fall on hard times."

"I will never complain about another thing because they have such a great attitude about life. Whether you're Oprah Winfrey, or just someone living in a hollow, the question is 'What are you willing to give to your family, to the community, to the planet?' "

WYOMING

From America Online, October 3, 1995, when asked, *Do you ever get tired of not having a private life?*

"Sometimes—but you would never believe what I did this weekend. It was Stedman's idea of fun. We went to Wyoming to the home of a friend of his and we herded cattle. For six hours yesterday my butt sat in the saddle following a thousand cows trying to get them to head east. What fun. Today I can hardly walk. But I don't believe the *Enquirer* was anywhere around. It was very private."

Trust

From *The Ed Gordon Show*, May 30, 1995, when asked whether she was hurt when folks she had been close to came out and said that she had changed and that things were different, and so on:

"It didn't hurt me, I will say this, let me see, Was I hurt? I can't use the word *hurt* actually.

Was she mad?

"Yeah, it really ticked me off because I thought, how dare you? That's what I thought. How dare you because I've been really good to you. I treated you like more than a friend and I've treated you with honor and I've done more, bent over backward and been more than fair, so how dare you tell that lie about me? That's how I felt, but I wasn't hurt by it. So I accept that as reality. So I said, 'Everybody do confidentiality agreements,' not that that's gonna really solve anything if somebody decides to betray you, 'and I mean everybody.' I mean everybody who comes in my house. If you bring flowers to my house, you gotta sign an agreement that says you're not gonna come in there with a camera. That's after my whole house ended up in the *National Enquirer*.

"And so it's made me less trustful of people. I will say that. I was hoping that this would not have happened to me. I was talking to Barbra Streisand about this, and she was saying, 'Don't you have confidentiality agreements?' And I go, 'Well, then, doesn't that make people feel like you don't trust them?' And she said, 'But you don't.' So I now moved to that ground. I never thought that I would."

"That used to be the thing: Oh, my God, do anything but go through your entire life and don't step on anybody's toes. Don't hurt anybody's feelings. Leave them all thinking that you're nice. Now I think, I know that I'm nice, if you don't think it, that's really okay. The bottom line is, sign the agreement."

Short Subjects

Truth

꧂

"One of the reasons I believe I have been able to achieve what I have is because I have sought truth in my life."

During her early days on TV, while reading the news, she mispronounced a word and laughed about it on the air—a big taboo at the time:

"It was the first time I had shown any resemblance to truth on the air. Before that I was a Twinkie doll. Everything was done for me—the script, how I should look, how I should talk. It was all, 'Thank you, Jerry, and now back to you, Bob.' I was *pretending* to be something. I wasn't real.

"When you're lying, your spirit is uncomfortable. I'm grateful for those years. I always knew it was a means to an end. But I couldn't be an objective anchor reading words written for me by someone else.

"I'm a truth seeker. That's what I do every day on the show—put out the truth. Some people don't like it, they call it sensational, but I say life is sensational."

"If you seek what is honorable, what is good, what is the truth of your life, all the other things you could not imagine come as a matter of course."

From a speech to AWED (American Woman's Economic Development Corporation), 1989:

"I was fat for a long time with Stedman. I decided to lose weight because for a long time I was tired of lying to myself. The weight was an untruth in my life. It served to block me, prohibit me from doing and feeling as good as I could. It stopped me doing things I felt I could do if I were a thinner person.

"Whatever it is that is blocking the truth in your life, you have to rid yourself of blocks and barriers before you can go on. I have found that I can fly, and that's because I got the weight, the garbage, out of my wings, because for me that was weighing me down."

Work

"My friends are the office people. We work and we go out to dinner and talk about work. Then we go home and we're back here about seven-thirty in the morning."

Asked if she's a workaholic:
"Yes, ma'am, I am. This is all I do. I do this and I do it till I drop. I work, and on weekends I go as many places as I can to speak.

I get home and I say, 'What am I supposed to do here? I guess I *could* go to the movies.' I could. I could do that. I don't."

1986

"I'm not a workaholic. I just do what seems to be important. Like the Nike ad, I 'just do it.' "

1990